MAYER SMITH

The Starwoven Bride

Copyright © 2025 by Mayer Smith

All rights reserved. No part of this publication may be reproduced, stored or transmitted in any form or by any means, electronic, mechanical, photocopying, recording, scanning, or otherwise without written permission from the publisher. It is illegal to copy this book, post it to a website, or distribute it by any other means without permission.

This novel is entirely a work of fiction. The names, characters and incidents portrayed in it are the work of the author's imagination. Any resemblance to actual persons, living or dead, events or localities is entirely coincidental.

Mayer Smith asserts the moral right to be identified as the author of this work.

Mayer Smith has no responsibility for the persistence or accuracy of URLs for external or third-party Internet Websites referred to in this publication and does not guarantee that any content on such Websites is, or will remain, accurate or appropriate.

Designations used by companies to distinguish their products are often claimed as trademarks. All brand names and product names used in this book and on its cover are trade names, service marks, trademarks and registered trademarks of their respective owners. The publishers and the book are not associated with any product or vendor mentioned in this book. None of the companies referenced within the book have endorsed the book.

First edition

*This book was professionally typeset on Reedsy.
Find out more at reedsy.com*

Contents

1	The Loom of Fate	1
2	The Masked Stranger	7
3	Secrets Beneath the Stars	13
4	The Whispered Threat	20
5	Shadows in the Palace	26
6	A Game of Veils	33
7	The Forbidden Garden	40
8	The Starwoven Legacy	47
9	Betrayal at Midnight	54
10	The Bond of Stars	60
11	The Dagger and the Dance	66
12	The Fading Star	73
13	The Silent Alliance	79
14	The Starborn Trials	86
15	A Web of Lies	93
16	The Celestial Betrayal	100
17	The Starlight Refuge	107
18	The Prophecy Unraveled	113
19	The Starwoven Crown	120
20	A Battle Under the Stars	127
21	The Choice of Eternity	133
22	The Starwoven Bride	139

One

The Loom of Fate

The sky above the small town of Erendale shimmered with an otherworldly brilliance. Stars sparkled like diamonds scattered across a velvet canvas, their light weaving intricate patterns that seemed almost deliberate. It was an unusual night, even for a town nestled at the edge of myths and legends. Tonight, the air itself seemed alive, heavy with the promise of change, though no one could quite put their finger on why.

Ellara bent over her loom, her fingers deftly working the wooden shuttle back and forth through the warp threads. The rhythmic clack of her weaving drowned out the world around her, a soothing metronome to the chaos of her thoughts. Her modest home, tucked away at the outskirts of the bustling marketplace, felt unusually quiet tonight. Even the chirping of crickets seemed to have stilled, leaving her alone with her restless mind.

The woven fabric under her hands shimmered faintly, its threads catching the light in a way that made it seem almost alive. Her clients always said she had a touch of magic in her work, though Ellara dismissed it as nothing more than skill honed by years of practice. Still, there was something about the fabric tonight, something she couldn't quite name. A shimmer that felt different, as if the stars themselves had blessed her creation.

A knock at the door startled her from her reverie. She glanced at the clock—well past midnight. Visitors at this hour were rare, and her heart quickened with a mix of curiosity and unease. Tightening her grip on the shuttle, she rose from her seat and crossed the small room, her bare feet brushing against the cold wooden floor.

"Who's there?" she called, her voice steadier than she felt.

Silence greeted her at first. Then, a deep, gravelly voice replied, "A friend. I mean no harm."

Ellara hesitated, her hand hovering over the latch. Something about the voice was both reassuring and unnerving. Finally, she opened the door just enough to peer outside.

A man stood there, cloaked in a dark, heavy garment that obscured most of his features. His face was hidden beneath the shadow of a hood, but his posture spoke of urgency. He held out a parchment, sealed with an emblem she didn't recognize—a star with threads spiraling outward.

"I was told to give this to you," he said, his tone low but insistent.

Ellara glanced at the parchment, then back at the man. "Who sent you?"

"I cannot say," he replied, his voice tinged with regret. "But you must read it. The stars have chosen you."

Before she could respond, he turned on his heel and disappeared into the night, his figure melting into the shadows as though he had never been there. Ellara stood frozen for a moment, the parchment clutched in her trembling hand. The stars have chosen you. The words echoed in her mind, leaving her both intrigued and uneasy.

Closing the door, she returned to her worktable and set the parchment down. The seal shimmered faintly in the lamplight, the intricate design almost hypnotic. Taking a deep breath, she broke it open and unrolled the parchment. The handwriting was elegant, the ink a deep, shimmering silver that caught the light as though it were alive.

To the Weaver of Fates,

The time has come. You are chosen to fulfill the prophecy woven into the stars. A union of unimaginable consequence awaits, one that will alter the course of kingdoms. Seek the Stargazer at the Northern Tower. Your answers lie there. But beware: the threads of fate are fragile, and not all who walk beneath the stars wish for their light to shine.

May the stars guide you.

The message ended abruptly, with no signature or indication of who had sent it. Ellara's hands shook as she set the parchment down, her heart pounding in her chest. The words were cryptic, yet their weight was undeniable. She was no stranger to tales of prophecies and stargazers—Erendale was steeped in such legends—but to be at the center of one? That was beyond anything she could have imagined.

Her thoughts were interrupted by a faint noise outside, a soft rustling like fabric brushing against stone. She turned toward the window, her pulse quickening. The town was still shrouded in silence, but her instincts told her she was not alone.

Slowly, she approached the window and peered out. At first, she saw nothing but the empty street bathed in moonlight. Then, a flicker of movement caught her eye—a figure standing at the edge of the shadows, watching her. The same hooded man? No, this one was taller, broader, and something about his stance radiated menace.

Ellara stepped back, her breath catching in her throat. Whoever this was, they weren't here to deliver cryptic messages. A flash of light caught her attention, and she realized the figure was holding something—metal, perhaps a dagger.

Panic surged through her, but years of living alone had taught her to think quickly. She grabbed a heavy wooden rod from beside the loom, her knuckles white as she gripped it tightly. The figure outside moved closer, their steps deliberate and unhurried.

"Leave," she called out, her voice firm despite the fear constricting her chest. "I don't know what you want, but you won't find it here."

The figure paused, tilting their head as though considering her words. Then, without a sound, they turned and disappeared into the shadows, leaving Ellara standing there, her heart racing and her mind spinning.

She locked the door and bolted it for good measure, her back pressed against the cool wood. The parchment on the table seemed to pulse with a strange energy, as though urging her to act. She didn't know who had sent the message or what dangers awaited her if she followed its instructions, but one thing was clear: her quiet life in Erendale had just unraveled, and there was no going back.

Turning to the parchment, she read the words again, committing them to memory. The Stargazer at the Northern Tower. That was her first clue, her first step into a mystery she couldn't yet fathom. Tomorrow, she would begin her journey. Tonight, she would weave her thoughts into the fabric of the stars, hoping they would guide her to whatever fate had in store.

As she returned to her loom, the stars outside seemed to burn brighter, their light weaving intricate patterns across the night sky. And for the first time, Ellara felt as though those patterns were speaking directly to her.

The Loom of Fate had begun to turn.

Two

The Masked Stranger

The sun rose reluctantly over Erendale, its golden rays filtering through a thin veil of clouds, as if uncertain about fully revealing itself. The town's marketplace, usually bustling by midmorning, was quieter than usual. Vendors muttered about the strange weather while setting up their stalls, their voices mingling with the clatter of crates and the occasional neigh of horses.

Ellara made her way through the winding streets, her hood drawn low to shield her face from the biting wind and prying eyes. Her satchel was slung across her shoulder, filled with rolls of her finest woven fabric. Today's market trip was both an obligation and a distraction, though her thoughts were far from her craft. The cryptic message she had received the night before weighed heavily on her mind. Every step she took seemed to echo with the words, Seek the Stargazer.

She reached the market square and set up her modest stall near the fountain, a central spot where foot traffic was heavy. Her hands moved automatically as she arranged the fabrics in neat, colorful rows, but her eyes darted constantly, scanning the faces around her. The figure from the night before still haunted her thoughts. Were they watching her now? Was she being followed?

"Lovely work, as always," a familiar voice interrupted her vigilance.

Ellara looked up to see Miriam, a plump, cheerful baker whose stall was directly across from hers. She forced a smile, grateful for the semblance of normalcy.

"Thank you, Miriam," she replied, her voice steady despite the unease simmering beneath the surface. "How's the bread today?"

"Fresh and warm, like always. You should stop by later and grab a loaf. On the house." Miriam's eyes twinkled with kindness, but her expression shifted to concern as she studied Ellara's face. "Are you all right, dear? You look pale."

"I'm fine," Ellara said quickly. "Just didn't sleep well."

Miriam nodded sympathetically and returned to her stall, leaving Ellara to her thoughts. She couldn't afford to let her guard down, not when something—or someone—seemed determined to unsettle her life.

The Masked Stranger

The morning passed uneventfully, save for the occasional customer who stopped to admire her fabrics. Ellara fell into the rhythm of bartering and selling, letting the familiar routine soothe her frayed nerves. But as the sun climbed higher, casting sharper shadows across the marketplace, a disturbance broke the calm.

It started as a low murmur, a ripple of unease that spread through the crowd. Heads turned toward the far end of the square, where a group of men had gathered, their voices raised in anger. Ellara squinted, trying to make out what was happening. Two figures stood at the center of the commotion, their postures tense. One was a burly man in a leather apron, his face flushed with rage. The other was a tall, lean figure cloaked in black, his face obscured by a silver mask.

"You think you can cheat me?" the man in the apron bellowed, jabbing a finger at the masked stranger. "I know your kind—slippery, full of tricks. Pay what you owe, or there'll be trouble."

The masked man said nothing, his silence only fueling the other's anger. The tension in the square was palpable as the crowd watched, torn between curiosity and caution.

Ellara felt a strange pull, an inexplicable need to move closer. Her feet carried her toward the scene before her mind could catch up, her heart pounding in her chest. There was something about the masked stranger that set him apart, something magnetic yet dangerous.

As she approached, the burly man lunged, his massive hands

reaching for the stranger. But the masked figure moved with startling agility, sidestepping the attack and twisting the man's arm behind his back in one fluid motion. The crowd gasped as the aggressor cried out in pain.

"Enough," the masked man said, his voice low and commanding. "I owe you nothing. Let this be the end of it."

The burly man stumbled back as the stranger released him, clutching his arm and muttering curses under his breath. The crowd began to disperse, the spectacle over, but Ellara remained rooted to the spot, her eyes fixed on the masked man.

He turned his head slightly, as if sensing her gaze. For a fleeting moment, their eyes met—or at least, she thought they did, though the mask obscured much of his face. There was an intensity in that brief connection, a silent exchange that left her breathless.

Before she could think of what to do or say, the masked man strode toward her, his movements purposeful yet unhurried. Ellara's pulse quickened as he stopped a few paces away, his presence commanding without being overtly threatening.

"You're not afraid," he said, his tone more curious than accusatory.

Ellara straightened, meeting his gaze as evenly as she could. "Should I be?"

A faint chuckle escaped him, low and rich like the distant

rumble of thunder. "Perhaps. Most people are."

"What do you want?" she asked, her voice steadier than she felt.

"That depends," he replied, tilting his head. "Do you believe in fate?"

The question caught her off guard. "Fate?"

"Yes. The invisible threads that bind us, that pull us toward certain moments, certain people." He gestured subtly toward her stall. "Your craft suggests you understand such things."

Ellara narrowed her eyes, suspicion flaring in her chest. "Who are you?"

"A wanderer. A seeker of answers," he said cryptically. "Much like yourself, I suspect."

His words sent a chill down her spine. How could he know anything about her? About the message, the prophecy? Her instincts screamed at her to demand answers, to uncover who—or what—he truly was, but something held her back. A sense that pushing too hard might unravel more than she was prepared to face.

"I don't know what you're talking about," she said, her voice edged with caution.

The masked man regarded her for a long moment, as if weighing her response. Finally, he nodded, as though reaching some unspoken conclusion. "Perhaps you don't. But you will."

Before she could respond, he turned and melted into the crowd, leaving her standing there with more questions than ever. She wanted to chase after him, to demand clarity, but her feet refused to move. The weight of his presence lingered, as if he had left a part of himself behind.

Ellara returned to her stall in a daze, her mind racing. Who was he? How did he know about her craft, her connection to the prophecy? And what did he mean by "you will"?

The rest of the day passed in a blur. By the time she packed up her fabrics and headed home, the sun was sinking low on the horizon, casting long shadows across the streets. The marketplace was emptying, but Ellara couldn't shake the feeling that she was being watched.

As she turned onto the quiet lane that led to her home, she glanced over her shoulder. The street behind her was empty, but the unease refused to leave her. Her thoughts drifted back to the masked stranger, his cryptic words echoing in her mind.

"Do you believe in fate?"

She didn't have an answer. Not yet. But she was beginning to suspect that fate, whatever it was, had its eyes firmly fixed on her.

The stars above flickered into view, their light dim and distant, yet somehow watching.

Three

Secrets Beneath the Stars

Night fell over Erendale, the kind of night that felt alive with whispers and possibilities. The stars blanketed the sky in dazzling patterns, their brilliance casting faint silvery hues across the rooftops and cobblestone streets. Ellara sat at her loom, her hands still but her mind racing. The events of the day—the masked stranger, his cryptic words, and the lingering sense that she was being watched—refused to leave her alone.

Her small home felt suffocating, the walls closing in around her as her thoughts churned. The parchment from the previous night lay folded on the table, its edges worn from her constant handling. Seek the Stargazer at the Northern Tower. The words pulled at her like a thread unraveling in her mind, tugging her toward something she didn't yet understand.

Ellara stood abruptly, the wooden chair scraping against the floor. Staying here felt unbearable. If she wasn't going to get any answers, she might as well clear her head. She grabbed her cloak, throwing it around her shoulders as she stepped out into the cool night.

The town was quieter than usual, the kind of quiet that made every sound seem magnified. Her footsteps echoed softly against the cobblestones as she made her way through the empty streets. She wasn't entirely sure where she was going—just that the stars above seemed to beckon her forward.

The marketplace, so lively during the day, was eerily still now, the stalls deserted and shrouded in shadows. A breeze swept through, rustling loose tarps and sending a chill down her spine. She paused in the center of the square, her gaze drifting upward to the stars. They seemed impossibly bright tonight, their light forming shapes and patterns that felt both familiar and strange.

"You feel it, don't you?"

The voice came from behind her, low and smooth like a whisper carried on the wind. Ellara spun around, her heart leaping into her throat. Standing in the shadows near the fountain was the masked stranger from earlier, his tall figure partially obscured by the darkness.

"Why are you following me?" she demanded, her voice sharper than she intended.

"I'm not following you," he said, stepping closer. The faint light of the stars glinted off his silver mask, highlighting the sharp angles of its design. "We're both being led by the same thing."

Ellara frowned, her hands balling into fists at her sides. "Stop speaking in riddles. What do you want?"

"I want answers," he replied, his tone calm but insistent. "Just like you."

His words gave her pause. He wasn't wrong—she did want answers. Desperately. But how could she trust someone who cloaked himself in mystery and seemed to know far more about her than he should?

"Who are you?" she asked, her voice quieter now, tinged with uncertainty.

The masked man tilted his head slightly, as if considering how much to reveal. "Someone searching for the truth," he said finally. "Someone who's been watching the stars for a long time."

Ellara's unease deepened. "You still haven't answered my question. Why do you know about me? My craft? The stars?"

"I know because the stars have whispered your name," he said, his voice dropping to a near-whisper. "And because your path is tied to mine, whether we like it or not."

The cryptic response sent a shiver down her spine. She wanted to dismiss his words as nonsense, but something about them resonated deep within her, stirring an instinct she couldn't ignore.

"What do you mean, tied to your path?" she asked, stepping closer despite herself.

"The prophecy," he said simply. "The one written in the stars."

Ellara's breath caught. The parchment. The message. The Stargazer. Everything she had tried to piece together now felt like fragments of a larger puzzle, one that this man seemed to hold more pieces of than she did.

"You know about the prophecy?" she asked, her voice barely above a whisper.

He nodded. "I've spent years studying it, searching for its meaning. And now, for reasons I don't yet fully understand, it's led me to you."

The weight of his words settled heavily on her chest. She wanted to believe he was lying, but the conviction in his tone was impossible to ignore.

"Why me?" she asked, the question tumbling out before she could stop it. "I'm just a weaver. I'm no one special."

The masked man chuckled softly, a sound that carried no humor. "The stars don't choose people at random. You're more special than you realize."

Ellara shook her head, taking a step back. "This doesn't make any sense."

"It will," he said. "But only if you're willing to see it."

Before she could respond, he turned and began walking toward the edge of the square. Ellara hesitated, torn between the desire to flee and the need to follow. Against her better judgment, she found herself moving after him, her curiosity outweighing her fear.

He led her through the winding streets of the town, his strides confident despite the darkness. The farther they went, the quieter the world seemed to become, as if the town itself were holding its breath. Finally, they reached a small clearing on the outskirts of Erendale, where the stars shone unobstructed by the glow of lanterns or the haze of smoke.

The masked man stopped and turned to face her. "Look up," he said.

Ellara frowned but complied, tilting her head back to gaze at the night sky. The stars were impossibly vivid here, their light forming intricate patterns that seemed almost deliberate. As she stared, she realized that some of the patterns were familiar—shapes she had seen in her dreams, in the fabrics she wove without understanding why.

"It's beautiful," she admitted, her voice soft.

"It's more than beautiful," he said. "It's a map."

"A map to what?"

"To the truth," he replied. "And to the answers you're seeking."

Ellara tore her gaze away from the stars to look at him. "What kind of truth?"

"The kind that changes everything," he said, his tone grave. "The kind that reveals who you truly are and why you've been chosen."

His words sent a chill through her, but before she could respond, a sudden rustling sound broke the stillness. Ellara's head snapped toward the treeline, her heart pounding. Shadows shifted among the trees, and the faint glint of metal caught her eye.

"We're not alone," the masked man said, his voice low but sharp. He moved in front of her, his posture tense.

"Who's there?" Ellara called out, her voice trembling.

Silence answered her at first, but then a figure emerged from the shadows—a man clad in dark armor, his face obscured by a hood. He carried a sword at his side, and his presence radiated menace.

"You've strayed too far, little weaver," the man said, his voice cold and mocking. "The stars can't protect you here."

Ellara's blood ran cold as the masked man stepped forward,

placing himself between her and the stranger. "Stay back," he warned, his voice low and dangerous.

The armored man chuckled. "You think you can stop me? You don't even know who you're dealing with."

Ellara's mind raced, her fear threatening to overwhelm her. But as she looked up at the stars, a strange calm settled over her. The patterns seemed to shift and dance, their light guiding her thoughts. She didn't know how she knew, but she was certain of one thing: this was only the beginning.

Four

The Whispered Threat

The early morning light struggled to pierce the heavy fog that had descended over Erendale, cloaking the town in an eerie stillness. The kind of stillness that made people instinctively lower their voices, as if the air itself had secrets to guard. Ellara woke with a start, her heart pounding and her breath shallow. She had dreamed again—fragmented images of stars spinning in an endless sky, threads weaving themselves into a tapestry she couldn't quite see. And always, in the distance, a whisper she couldn't understand.

Shaking off the remnants of sleep, she rose from her bed and crossed the small room to the table where the parchment lay. Its presence felt heavier now, as though the weight of its words had grown overnight. She hadn't told anyone about it, not even Miriam, though her friend had noticed her distracted demeanor at the market the day before. There was no one she could trust with something like this. Not yet.

Her fingers brushed the edge of the parchment as a sharp knock shattered the morning's silence. Ellara froze, her breath catching in her throat. Visitors were rare this early, and after her encounter with the masked stranger, her nerves were frayed. The knock came again, louder this time, impatient.

Cautiously, she moved to the door, her heart pounding. "Who is it?" she called, her voice trembling despite her attempt to sound steady.

"A message," came the reply, the voice low and unfamiliar.

Ellara hesitated, her hand hovering over the latch. The last messenger who had come to her door had left her with more questions than answers. Finally, she cracked the door open, keeping the chain in place. A young boy stood on the other side, his face smudged with dirt and his clothes worn but serviceable. He held out a small folded note, his expression blank.

"This is for you," he said simply.

Ellara unlatched the chain and took the note, glancing at the boy. "Who sent you?"

"I don't know," he said, already turning to leave. "It was left at the inn this morning with your name on it."

She watched him disappear into the fog before retreating into her home and bolting the door. Unfolding the note, she felt a chill run through her. The handwriting was sharp and precise, each letter etched as if with purpose:

Leave Erendale. The stars may guide, but they cannot protect. You've been marked, and the threads are fraying. If you value your life, you'll go.

No signature, no seal. Just a stark warning that sent a cold knot of fear twisting in her stomach. Her first instinct was to dismiss it as an empty threat, a cruel joke by someone who had caught wind of the prophecy. But deep down, she knew better. The message felt personal, its tone intimate, as though the writer knew far more about her than they should.

Her thoughts were interrupted by a faint sound outside—a soft scrape, like a boot scuffing against stone. She froze, her ears straining. The sound came again, closer this time. Someone was out there.

Moving quickly, she snuffed out the lamp and pressed herself against the wall, her eyes trained on the window. The fog blurred the view, but she could just make out a shadow moving past, deliberate and slow. Whoever it was wasn't in a hurry. They were searching.

Ellara's pulse thundered in her ears as she reached for the wooden rod she kept by the loom, her only makeshift weapon. The shadow lingered by the window, then moved toward the door. Her grip tightened as the door rattled softly, a hand testing the latch. Locked.

She held her breath, praying the intruder would leave. But then came a soft, deliberate knock, followed by a voice—a voice she recognized all too well.

"Ellara," the masked stranger called, his tone low but urgent. "Open the door. We need to talk."

Her grip on the rod loosened slightly, but her wariness didn't fade. How had he found her? And why was he here now, when danger seemed to lurk around every corner?

"What do you want?" she asked, not moving from her spot against the wall.

"To keep you alive," he replied, his voice calm but firm. "You're in more danger than you realize."

She hesitated, the warning note still clutched in her hand. "How do I know I can trust you?"

"You don't," he admitted. "But I've risked exposing myself to come here, which should tell you how serious this is."

Ellara considered his words, her mind racing. Finally, she unbolted the door and opened it just enough to let him slip inside. He moved quickly, closing the door behind him and securing the lock. His silver mask caught the faint light filtering through the curtains, a stark contrast to the darkness of his cloak.

"You've been marked," he said without preamble, his gaze

dropping to the note in her hand. "They know who you are."

"Who?" she demanded, her frustration bubbling to the surface. "Who's after me, and why?"

He stepped closer, his voice dropping to a near-whisper. "The Watchers. They're an order that's been guarding the secrets of the stars for centuries. And now they think you're a threat."

Ellara frowned, the name unfamiliar. "Why would they see me as a threat? I'm no one."

"You're the Weaver," he said, as though that explained everything. "The prophecy speaks of a weaver who will unravel the hidden threads of fate and reshape the destiny of kingdoms. They believe you're that person."

She shook her head, disbelief warring with fear. "This is ridiculous. I'm just a weaver. A simple craftswoman. Why would anyone think I'm capable of something like that?"

"Because the stars have chosen you," he said, his tone unwavering. "And whether you believe it or not, they see you as a danger. That's why you need to leave Erendale. Staying here is too great a risk."

Ellara's grip tightened on the note as she stared at him, her mind spinning. Leaving Erendale meant abandoning everything she had ever known—her home, her livelihood, her friends. But staying meant facing enemies she didn't understand, enemies who seemed determined to stop her at any cost.

"Where would I even go?" she asked, her voice barely above a whisper.

"To the Northern Tower," he said. "To the Stargazer. They'll have the answers you need."

The Northern Tower. The name sent a shiver through her, conjuring images of dark forests and treacherous paths. It was said to lie beyond the mountains, a place few dared to venture.

"And you?" she asked, narrowing her eyes at him. "Why are you helping me?"

He hesitated, the pause filled with unspoken weight. "Because our fates are tied, whether we like it or not. If you fall, so do I."

His words only deepened the mystery surrounding him, but before she could press further, another sound shattered the quiet—a faint thud, followed by the creak of wood. Both of them froze, their eyes locking.

"They're here," he said, his voice barely audible. "We need to go. Now."

Ellara's heart raced as she grabbed her cloak and the note, her mind a whirlwind of fear and questions. Together, they slipped out the back door and into the fog, the shadows of the Watchers closing in behind them.

Five

Shadows in the Palace

The sprawling palace loomed over the capital city like a guardian, its towering spires piercing the sky and its stone walls whispering of centuries-old secrets. Ellara stood at the edge of the bustling palace grounds, her heart pounding in her chest. She had never been this close to such grandeur, and the sheer scale of it made her feel small and insignificant. The opulent gates, gilded with intricate carvings of celestial patterns, seemed to mock her with their impenetrability.

"This is a mistake," she whispered, clutching her cloak tighter around her. The hood concealed her face, but her trembling hands betrayed her unease.

The masked stranger, standing at her side, cast her a sharp glance. "It's not a mistake. It's necessary. You need to see what's inside."

Ellara swallowed hard, her gaze shifting to the crowds of nobles and servants bustling in and out of the palace gates. The upcoming banquet had drawn attendees from across the kingdom, and the palace grounds were alive with activity. Carriages rolled up the cobblestone paths, their occupants dressed in fine silks and glittering jewels. Guards patrolled the area, their eyes scanning the crowds with practiced precision.

"How do we even get in?" she asked, her voice barely audible over the din.

The stranger reached into his cloak and produced a small, ornate medallion. "With this," he said, holding it up for her to see. The medallion bore the royal crest—a sun encircled by a ring of stars—and its craftsmanship was exquisite. "This will grant us access, but you'll need to keep your head down. We can't risk being recognized."

Ellara frowned, doubt gnawing at her. "Recognized by who? No one here knows me."

He gave her a pointed look. "Not yet. But trust me, there are eyes everywhere in this palace. And some of them have been watching you for a long time."

The cryptic warning sent a shiver down her spine, but she nodded, swallowing her fear. Together, they joined the flow of people heading toward the gates. As they approached, the stranger handed the medallion to a guard, who scrutinized it before nodding and stepping aside. Ellara felt a surge of relief as they passed through the gates, but it was short-lived. The palace courtyard was even more intimidating up close, its grandeur overwhelming.

The stranger led her through the throng of people, his movements purposeful and assured. Ellara followed closely, her eyes darting nervously as they passed courtiers and servants. She caught snippets of conversations—discussions of trade agreements, gossip about noble families, speculation about the banquet. It all felt so far removed from her world, yet here she was, an outsider in the heart of it all.

They entered the main hall, and Ellara couldn't suppress a gasp. The space was breathtaking, with vaulted ceilings adorned with murals of constellations and chandeliers dripping with crystal. The floor was polished to a mirror-like shine, reflecting the light in a dazzling display. Servants moved with practiced efficiency, setting tables with silverware and arranging elaborate floral centerpieces.

"Keep moving," the stranger murmured, nudging her forward.

He guided her toward a side corridor, away from the main hall. The opulence of the palace began to fade as they ventured deeper, replaced by narrower passageways lit by flickering torches. The air grew cooler, and the faint hum of conversation from the banquet preparations faded into an unsettling silence.

"Where are we going?" Ellara asked, her voice hushed.

"To the archives," the stranger replied. "If there's any record of the prophecy—or why they're after you—it'll be there."

Ellara's unease deepened. The archives sounded like the kind of place she had no business being, and the idea of sneaking into it sent her pulse racing. "And what happens if we're caught?"

The stranger didn't answer, his silence more unnerving than any response he could have given.

The corridor ended at a heavy wooden door, its surface carved with intricate patterns of stars and moons. The stranger produced a small key and inserted it into the lock, the mechanism clicking softly. He pushed the door open, revealing a dimly lit room lined with shelves that stretched from floor to ceiling. Each shelf was packed with scrolls, tomes, and ledgers, their spines marked with faded symbols.

Ellara hesitated on the threshold, the weight of the room pressing down on her. "This feels… forbidden."

"It is," the stranger said bluntly, stepping inside. "But that's never stopped me before."

Reluctantly, she followed him, her eyes scanning the shelves. The room smelled of aged parchment and dust, a testament to its centuries-old contents. The stranger moved with purpose, pulling books from the shelves and flipping through them with practiced efficiency.

"What exactly are we looking for?" she asked, her voice barely above a whisper.

"Anything that mentions the Weaver," he said without looking up. "The prophecy, the Watchers, the stars—anything that connects the dots."

Ellara nodded, though she felt woefully out of her depth. She began scanning the shelves, her fingers trailing over the spines of ancient tomes. The symbols meant nothing to her, and the sheer volume of information was overwhelming.

As she reached for a particularly ornate book, a faint sound caught her attention—a soft creak, like a floorboard shifting. She froze, her hand hovering over the book. The stranger noticed her stillness and looked up, his body instantly tensing.

"What is it?" he asked.

"I heard something," she whispered, her voice trembling.

The stranger moved to her side, his eyes scanning the room. "Stay here," he said, his tone leaving no room for argument.

Ellara nodded, clutching her cloak tightly as he moved toward the door. He opened it cautiously, peering into the corridor. For a moment, there was only silence. Then, without warning, a shadow moved—a guard, stepping into view with a hand on his sword.

The stranger reacted instantly, slamming the door shut and locking it. "We've been found," he said, his voice tight. "They must have followed us."

Panic surged through Ellara. "What do we do?"

He moved quickly, grabbing a stack of books and shoving them into his satchel. "We need to get out of here. Now."

The sound of boots echoed down the corridor, growing louder with each passing second. Ellara's heart pounded as she followed the stranger to the back of the room, where a narrow staircase spiraled upward.

"This leads to the servants' quarters," he explained. "If we're lucky, we can slip out unnoticed."

They ascended the stairs quickly, the sound of their footsteps drowned out by the approaching guards. Ellara's legs burned with the effort, but fear propelled her forward. When they reached the top, the stranger pushed open a small hatch, revealing a dimly lit hallway.

"Go," he urged, helping her through the opening.

They moved swiftly down the hallway, their footsteps muffled by the worn carpet. Ellara's mind raced, her thoughts a jumble of fear and questions. Who had discovered them? How much did they know? And most importantly, what would happen if they were caught?

The sound of voices behind them spurred her onward, her breath coming in short, panicked gasps. The stranger led her to a narrow window and opened it, revealing the palace gardens below.

"Climb down," he said, gesturing to the ivy-covered wall. "I'll be right behind you."

Ellara hesitated, the drop making her stomach churn. But there was no time to argue. She gripped the ivy tightly and began her descent, her hands trembling as she searched for footholds. The stranger followed, his movements far more practiced and assured.

When they reached the ground, he grabbed her arm and pulled her into the shadows of the garden. The voices of the guards were faint now, but they couldn't afford to linger. Together, they slipped through the palace gates and disappeared into the night.

Ellara's heart was still racing when they finally stopped in the safety of a secluded alley. She turned to the stranger, her fear giving way to anger. "What just happened? Who were those guards?"

"The Watchers," he said grimly. "They know you're here. And now, they'll stop at nothing to find you."

Ellara's blood ran cold. The shadows in the palace had been more than just an ominous presence—they had been a warning. A warning that her life, and the secrets she carried, were in greater danger than ever before.

Six

A Game of Veils

The grand ballroom of the palace was a marvel of gilded splendor. Crystal chandeliers hung like frozen constellations, their light casting prismatic reflections over polished marble floors. Musicians in the gallery played a hauntingly beautiful melody, weaving a tapestry of sound that filled the air with a sense of opulence and anticipation. The crowd, adorned in silks and jewels, moved gracefully through the space, their laughter and chatter a gentle hum beneath the music.

Ellara stood near the edge of the ballroom, her heart pounding as she gripped the delicate folds of her borrowed gown. It was a deep sapphire blue, chosen by the masked stranger to complement her dark eyes and blend with the midnight tones of the evening. A sheer veil concealed her face, her features hidden just enough to provide a layer of anonymity among the glittering crowd. Her hair, swept into an elegant twist, completed the transformation from humble weaver to mysterious noblewoman.

But the illusion was fragile. Every step she took felt like walking a tightrope, every glance in her direction a potential threat. The weight of the prophecy, the Watchers, and the danger that loomed over her seemed to press against her chest, making it difficult to breathe.

"Remember," the masked stranger had told her earlier, his voice low and firm. "Blend in. Speak as little as possible. Let them underestimate you."

Now, as she stood among the kingdom's elite, those words felt like a lifeline. The stranger was somewhere in the ballroom, his face concealed by one of the many masks that dotted the crowd. He had insisted on her attendance, claiming that this was the best chance to gather information about the Watchers and their plans. But as Ellara surveyed the room, the enormity of the task ahead overwhelmed her.

The air grew heavier as a tall man entered the ballroom, his presence commanding instant attention. Duke Marcellus, one of the most powerful figures in the kingdom, strode confidently through the crowd, his silver hair glinting under the chandeliers. His piercing blue eyes swept the room, and for a moment, they seemed to linger on Ellara. She stiffened, her hand tightening around the stem of her goblet. Was it her imagination, or did he know something?

A soft voice broke through her tension. "You look nervous, my dear."

Ellara turned to find a woman standing beside her, dressed in a stunning crimson gown. Her auburn hair was piled high, and her lips curved into a smile that didn't quite reach her sharp green eyes. The woman's gaze flitted over Ellara's gown and veil, assessing her with the practiced ease of someone accustomed to weighing others' worth.

"I'm not used to such grandeur," Ellara replied, keeping her tone polite but distant.

The woman chuckled, a low, melodic sound. "Few are. But one must learn quickly if they wish to survive here."

Ellara forced a smile, her mind racing. Who was this woman, and why had she approached her? Before she could probe further, the woman leaned in slightly, her voice dropping to a conspiratorial whisper.

"Be careful," she said. "This ball may appear to be a celebration, but it's a hunting ground. The predators are watching."

Ellara's blood ran cold as the woman drifted away, her crimson gown swaying like a flame in the wind. The cryptic warning echoed in her mind, amplifying her unease. She scanned the crowd, searching for the masked stranger, but the sea of faces and glittering masks made it impossible to spot him.

Taking a steadying breath, Ellara moved toward the edge of

the room, where a row of towering arched windows offered a view of the moonlit gardens. The cool night air seeped through the glass, a welcome reprieve from the oppressive heat of the ballroom. She placed her goblet on a nearby table, her hands trembling slightly.

"You look out of place."

The voice startled her, smooth and rich, with a hint of amusement. Ellara turned to find a man standing nearby, dressed in a dark suit embroidered with silver thread. His face was obscured by a black mask adorned with small diamonds that sparkled like stars. His presence was imposing, yet there was an air of intrigue about him.

"I don't believe we've met," the man said, inclining his head. "I'm Lord Tavian."

Ellara's pulse quickened. She hadn't anticipated being approached so directly. She dipped into a shallow curtsey, recalling the etiquette lessons the stranger had hastily given her. "A pleasure, my lord."

Tavian's gaze lingered on her veil, his eyes sharp and calculating. "You're not like the others here," he remarked. "You don't seek the spotlight, yet you draw it nonetheless."

"I prefer to observe," Ellara replied carefully. "There's much to learn in silence."

He smiled faintly, though it didn't reach his eyes. "Wise words.

But in this court, silence can be dangerous. One must tread carefully, especially if they carry secrets."

The veiled threat in his words made Ellara's stomach churn. Before she could respond, a commotion drew their attention. The music had stopped, and the crowd parted as a figure stepped into the center of the ballroom. It was Duke Marcellus, his commanding presence silencing the room.

"Ladies and gentlemen," he began, his voice resonating with authority. "Tonight, we celebrate not just our kingdom's prosperity, but the unity that binds us. However, unity cannot exist without trust."

Ellara's heart pounded as Marcellus's gaze swept the room, his words heavy with implication. "There are whispers of unrest, of individuals who seek to disrupt the balance we have worked so hard to maintain. Let this be a reminder that the crown sees all."

The crowd murmured uneasily, and Ellara felt the weight of countless eyes shifting, searching for signs of weakness or guilt. Tavian leaned closer, his voice a low murmur. "He's not just talking about rebellion. He's hunting someone."

Ellara's hands clenched at her sides. Was Marcellus referring to her? To the prophecy? She forced herself to remain still, her face hidden behind the veil, even as fear threatened to consume her.

The music resumed, but the atmosphere remained tense.

Tavian excused himself, leaving Ellara alone once more. She moved toward the shadows near the windows, her breath coming in shallow gasps. The ball was becoming a trap, a gilded cage that tightened around her with every passing moment.

A hand brushed her arm, and she spun around, ready to flee. But it was the masked stranger, his expression hidden but his posture urgent.

"We need to leave," he said, his voice low. "Now."

"What's happening?" she asked, her voice barely above a whisper.

"They know you're here," he replied, his tone grim. "Marcellus is testing the waters, but it won't be long before they act."

Ellara nodded, her heart racing. Together, they slipped through the crowd, careful to avoid drawing attention. The masked stranger led her toward a side door, but before they could reach it, a voice rang out.

"Stop them!"

Guards emerged from the shadows, their swords gleaming in the light. The crowd gasped as the stranger pulled Ellara behind him, his hand dropping to the hilt of his concealed blade.

"Run," he hissed.

Ellara hesitated for only a moment before obeying, her skirts billowing as she darted toward the exit. The sound of clashing steel and shouts filled the air as the stranger held off their pursuers. She didn't look back, her focus fixed on the doorway ahead.

Bursting into the moonlit gardens, she sprinted toward the trees, her breath coming in ragged gasps. The shadows of the palace loomed behind her, but she didn't stop until she was deep within the forest. Only then did she collapse against a tree, her heart pounding and her mind racing.

The ball had been a game of veils, but the masks had fallen. And now, the hunt had truly begun.

Seven

The Forbidden Garden

The forest surrounding the palace had long been shrouded in whispers, tales of its unnatural stillness and the secrets hidden within its shadowy depths. The locals called it the Forbidden Garden—a place where the veil between the mortal world and the unknown was said to be perilously thin. For Ellara, it was now both a sanctuary and a labyrinth. The chill of the night air bit at her exposed skin as she crouched behind a dense thicket, her breaths shallow and rapid. The distant shouts of the palace guards reverberated through the trees, a stark reminder that her escape was far from secure.

Moonlight filtered through the tangled canopy above, casting faint silver streaks onto the forest floor. Every rustle of leaves and snap of twigs set her nerves on edge. She clutched the folds of her gown tightly, her fingers trembling as she tried to quiet the pounding of her heart.

"Ellara."

The whispered voice was barely audible, but it pierced through the night like a blade. She froze, her muscles tensing as her eyes darted toward the sound. Emerging from the shadows was the masked stranger, his figure a silhouette against the pale glow of the moon. Relief washed over her, though it was quickly tempered by the urgency etched into his movements.

"We have to keep moving," he said, his voice low but firm. "They're sweeping the outer perimeter. If they find us—"

"Why are they chasing me?" Ellara interrupted, her voice rising despite herself. "What do they want?"

The stranger hesitated, his gaze flickering toward the direction of the guards' distant voices. "This isn't the time for answers," he said, his tone clipped. "But I promise, you'll have them soon. Now, come."

Ellara bit back her frustration and followed him, her steps as silent as she could manage. The forest seemed to close in around them, the trees like looming sentinels guarding their secrets. The stranger moved with practiced ease, his movements swift and deliberate, while Ellara struggled to keep up, her gown snagging on brambles and her shoes sinking into the damp earth.

They came upon a clearing, its center dominated by an ancient stone fountain. The structure was weathered with age, its edges chipped and overgrown with moss, but the faint trickle of water still flowed from its spout. The air here felt heavier, charged with an energy that made Ellara's skin prickle. She paused, her gaze drawn to the fountain's basin. The water reflected the moonlight in an unnatural way, its surface shimmering as though it held the stars themselves.

"This way," the stranger urged, but Ellara lingered, her curiosity piqued despite her fear.

"There's something... different about this place," she murmured, stepping closer to the fountain. The air grew cooler the nearer she came, the faint hum of energy growing stronger.

The stranger turned back, his expression hidden behind his mask, but his posture radiated tension. "Ellara, we don't have time for this."

Ignoring his warning, she reached out, her fingers brushing the water's surface. The moment she made contact, a vision burst into her mind—flashes of stars spinning in a vortex, threads of light weaving intricate patterns, and a figure cloaked in darkness standing at the center. The vision ended as abruptly as it began, leaving her breathless and disoriented.

"What was that?" she gasped, stumbling back.

The stranger caught her arm, steadying her. "You felt it, didn't you? The power of this place."

The Forbidden Garden

Ellara nodded, her voice trembling. "What is it?"

"The Forbidden Garden isn't just a name," he said, his tone grim. "This forest is older than the palace itself, older than the kingdom. It's tied to the stars, to the prophecy. That fountain is a focal point of its power."

Ellara stared at him, her mind reeling. "Why didn't you tell me?"

"Because knowing wouldn't have changed anything," he replied. "And because it's dangerous to linger here. The Watchers know about this place, and they'll be looking for you."

As if on cue, the sound of voices grew louder, closer. The guards were closing in. The stranger's grip on her arm tightened. "We need to move. Now."

This time, Ellara didn't argue. They plunged back into the forest, their path lit only by the faint glow of the moon. The stranger led her through a maze of twisting trails and dense undergrowth, his movements quick and assured. Ellara struggled to keep up, her lungs burning with the effort.

Just as the voices seemed to fade, the ground beneath her feet shifted. She let out a startled cry as the earth gave way, her body tumbling down a hidden slope. The world spun around her, dirt and leaves scraping against her skin as she fell. When she finally came to a stop, the air was knocked from her lungs, leaving her gasping and disoriented.

"Ellara!" the stranger's voice called, distant but urgent.

"I'm here," she managed to croak, pushing herself up. She winced as pain flared in her ankle—a sharp, twisting ache that made it difficult to stand.

The stranger appeared moments later, his figure emerging from the shadows like a wraith. He crouched beside her, his hands gentle as he examined her injury. "It's sprained," he said. "You won't be able to run."

Panic flared in her chest. "What do we do? They're still after us."

The stranger was silent for a moment, his gaze scanning their surroundings. They had landed in a hollow, the walls of earth and stone forming a natural barrier around them. Above, the trees formed a dense canopy, their branches entwined like the threads of a tapestry.

"There's a way out," he said finally, his voice steady. "But you'll need to trust me."

Ellara met his gaze, the weight of his words sinking in. "I don't have much of a choice, do I?"

He smiled faintly, though it didn't reach his eyes. "Not really."

He helped her to her feet, his arm supporting her as they moved deeper into the hollow. The path was narrow and uneven, but the stranger guided her with care, his movements deliberate

The Forbidden Garden

and sure. The air grew cooler as they descended, the faint sound of water echoing in the distance.

They reached a small underground stream, its crystal-clear waters flowing over smooth stones. The stranger knelt beside it, dipping his fingers into the water. He muttered something under his breath—a language Ellara didn't recognize—and the air seemed to shift.

"What are you doing?" she asked, her voice barely above a whisper.

"Opening the way," he replied.

The stream began to glow, its light spreading along the water's path and illuminating a hidden passageway. The stranger turned to her, his expression unreadable behind his mask. "This will take us to safety. But once we step through, there's no turning back."

Ellara hesitated, her gaze shifting between him and the glowing passage. She thought of the prophecy, the Watchers, the vision she had seen in the fountain. Everything in her life had led to this moment, this choice. Taking a deep breath, she nodded.

"Let's go."

The stranger extended his hand, and she took it, allowing him to guide her into the passage. The light of the stream surrounded them, its glow washing away the darkness. For the first time since this ordeal began, Ellara felt a flicker of hope. But deep in her heart, she knew the Forbidden Garden hadn't revealed all its secrets—and that the shadows they left behind would follow them into the light.

Eight

The Starwoven Legacy

The soft glow of dawn bathed the hidden passageway in muted shades of gray and gold as Ellara and the masked stranger emerged into a secluded glade. The world around them seemed untouched by time, a realm of ethereal beauty that felt both otherworldly and ancient. Towering trees stretched skyward, their branches entwined like protective arms shielding the secrets of the forest. A gentle mist curled around their feet, and the air carried the faint scent of earth and blooming wildflowers.

Ellara's steps faltered as her ankle throbbed with each movement, but the stranger's steady arm at her side kept her upright. She glanced at him, his mask still concealing his expression, yet his movements carried an air of urgency. He hadn't spoken much since they left the underground stream, and his silence only heightened her sense of foreboding.

"Where are we?" she asked, her voice breaking the stillness.

"A sanctuary," he replied. "For now."

The glade was dominated by a massive stone arch, its surface etched with intricate carvings of stars, moons, and swirling patterns that seemed to shimmer faintly in the early light. At its base, a circular dais lay partially buried in moss, its edges worn smooth by centuries of wind and rain. The archway hummed with an almost imperceptible energy, its presence both awe-inspiring and unsettling.

Ellara's gaze was drawn to the carvings. They were eerily familiar, echoing the designs she often wove into her fabrics without understanding why. Her fingers itched to trace the patterns, but she hesitated, unsure if touching the ancient stone would invoke some unknown power.

"This place," she murmured, "it feels… alive."

"It is," the stranger said, his tone reverent. "The Starwoven Arch. It's one of the few remnants of your ancestors' legacy."

Ellara turned to him sharply. "My ancestors?"

He nodded, his gaze fixed on the arch. "Your bloodline is tied to the stars, Ellara. The prophecy, the Watchers, everything—it all starts here."

Her mind reeled. She had always considered herself ordinary, a simple weaver with no remarkable heritage. The idea that her bloodline was somehow connected to the ancient powers she had been thrust into seemed impossible.

"That can't be true," she said, shaking her head. "My parents were farmers. They never spoke of anything like this."

"They wouldn't have known," he said gently. "Your lineage was hidden, buried under generations of obscurity to protect it. But the stars never forget."

Ellara's legs felt weak, and she sank onto the edge of the dais, her hands gripping the cool stone for support. "What does that even mean? What am I supposed to do with this… legacy?"

The stranger crouched beside her, his voice low and steady. "The Starwoven Arch is a gateway, a connection to the truths hidden in the stars. It holds the knowledge of your ancestors—the weavers who could shape fate itself."

She stared at him, her heart pounding. "Shape fate? That's just a story. A myth."

"It's more than a myth," he said, his tone firm. "You've felt it, haven't you? In your work. The way your hands move as though guided by something beyond yourself. The patterns you weave, the visions you've seen—they're all echoes of the power you carry."

Ellara couldn't deny the truth in his words. She had always felt an inexplicable connection to her craft, a sense that her hands were guided by something greater than her own skill. But to think that it was tied to an ancient power, to a legacy that could shape the course of fate—it was too much to comprehend.

The stranger stood, extending a hand toward the arch. "If you want answers, they're here. The arch will reveal them to you."

Ellara hesitated, fear and curiosity warring within her. "What if I'm not ready?"

"You don't have a choice," he said, his voice soft but unyielding. "The Watchers won't stop hunting you. The only way to survive this is to embrace what you are."

Taking a deep breath, Ellara pushed herself to her feet and approached the arch. The carvings seemed to pulse faintly, as though responding to her presence. She reached out, her fingertips grazing the cool stone. The moment she made contact, a surge of energy coursed through her, and the world around her blurred.

She was no longer in the glade. Instead, she stood in a vast expanse of starlight, the ground beneath her feet a swirling mosaic of constellations. Threads of light wove through the air, forming intricate patterns that shimmered and shifted with a life of their own. The air was alive with a low hum, a symphony of whispers that seemed to speak directly to her soul.

"Ellara."

The voice was soft yet commanding, and she turned to see a figure emerging from the starlight. It was a woman, her form both solid and ethereal, her features strikingly similar to Ellara's own. She wore a gown woven from starlight, its fabric shifting and flowing like water.

"Who are you?" Ellara asked, her voice trembling.

The woman smiled gently. "I am your ancestor, one of the first Starweavers. My name has been lost to time, but my essence remains here, within the threads."

Ellara's breath caught in her throat. "Why am I here?"

"Because the stars have chosen you to carry on our legacy," the woman said. "The power of the Starwoven Line has awakened in you, and with it comes great responsibility."

"I don't understand," Ellara said, her voice breaking. "I didn't ask for this. I don't want it."

"Fate rarely cares for what we want," the woman replied, her tone tinged with sadness. "But it is not a burden you carry alone. The threads of fate are woven by many hands. Yours is simply the one that holds the loom."

Ellara shook her head, tears pricking at her eyes. "I don't know how to do this. I'm not strong enough."

"You are," the woman said firmly. "You have always been strong, even when you didn't realize it. The power within you is not something you must earn—it is something you already possess. All you need to do is accept it."

Ellara hesitated, the weight of her fear and self-doubt pressing down on her. But as she looked into the woman's eyes, she saw a reflection of her own struggles and strength. Taking a deep breath, she nodded.

"What do I have to do?" she asked.

The woman stepped closer, placing a hand over Ellara's heart. "The first step is understanding. The threads will guide you, revealing the truths hidden in the stars. But beware—the more you learn, the more the Watchers will fear you. They will stop at nothing to destroy what they cannot control."

Ellara nodded, determination hardening her resolve. "Then I'll fight. I'll protect this legacy."

The woman smiled, pride shining in her eyes. "Good. Remember, Ellara, the stars are not your masters—they are your allies. Trust them, and trust yourself."

The vision began to fade, the starlight dimming as the whispers grew fainter. Ellara's surroundings shifted, and she found herself back in the glade, her hand still resting on the arch. The masked stranger stood nearby, his gaze fixed on her with an intensity that made her wonder if he had seen what she had.

"What did you see?" he asked.

Ellara turned to him, her voice steady despite the whirlwind of emotions within her. "The truth. And I'm ready."

But deep down, she knew that the path ahead would test her in ways she couldn't yet imagine—and that the legacy she had inherited would come at a cost.

Nine

Betrayal at Midnight

The night sky over Erendale was cloudless, the stars glittering like shards of ice against a backdrop of infinite black. The cold wind carried a sharp bite, rattling the treetops and whispering through the cracks of the crumbling walls surrounding the abandoned chapel where Ellara and the masked stranger had taken refuge. The air felt heavy, charged with a tension that Ellara couldn't shake.

She sat cross-legged on the stone floor, the glow of a single lantern casting flickering shadows across the dusty room. The faint scent of mildew and decayed wood filled her nose, mingling with the distant howls of the wind outside. Her hands trembled as she traced the patterns on the starwoven medallion the stranger had given her earlier—a relic he claimed was essential to unlocking the full truth of the prophecy.

"Why here?" she asked, her voice cutting through the oppressive silence. "Why this place?"

The masked stranger stood near the boarded-up window, his posture tense as he peered through a gap in the wood. The soft moonlight illuminated the edges of his figure, highlighting the sharp angles of his mask. He didn't turn to face her.

"Because it's hidden," he said finally. "The Watchers won't expect us to be this close to the palace."

Ellara frowned, her unease growing. "That's not what I meant. There's something about this place… something wrong."

The stranger turned, his gaze locking onto hers. "It's the history," he said, his voice quieter now. "This chapel was once a sanctuary for the Starweavers. A place where they gathered, where they shared their knowledge and wove the threads of fate. But when the Watchers rose to power, it became a graveyard."

Ellara shivered, glancing around the room. The walls bore faint carvings, their edges worn by time but still recognizable as the same starwoven patterns she had seen in her visions. A chill crept down her spine as the realization sank in—she was surrounded by the echoes of her ancestors, their legacy etched into the very stone.

Before she could respond, the stranger crossed the room and crouched beside her. His movements were deliberate, his presence commanding yet oddly comforting. "Are you ready?" he asked, his tone soft but firm.

Ellara tightened her grip on the medallion, her pulse quickening. "For what?"

"To confront the truth," he said. "The medallion holds the key to the prophecy's full meaning, but it requires your will to activate it. Once you do, there's no turning back."

The weight of his words settled heavily on her chest. She had come so far, endured so much, yet the path ahead felt darker and more treacherous than ever. But deep down, she knew there was no alternative. The Watchers would not stop, and the only way to survive was to face the prophecy head-on.

"I'm ready," she said, though her voice wavered.

The stranger nodded and stepped back, giving her space. Ellara took a deep breath and closed her eyes, focusing on the medallion's cool metal against her palm. The carvings seemed to hum faintly, their energy growing stronger as she concentrated. Slowly, she began to feel a pull, as though the medallion was reaching into her very soul.

The room around her seemed to dissolve, replaced by a swirling expanse of starlight. Threads of light wove through the void, forming intricate patterns that shifted and shimmered. At the center of it all was the prophecy—an image of a weaver standing before a loom of stars, her hands guiding threads that connected to every corner of the kingdom.

But the vision was not serene. Shadows loomed at the edges, twisting and writhing as they sought to tear the threads apart.

Betrayal at Midnight

Ellara felt their malice, their hunger to destroy what she represented. And then she saw him—a figure cloaked in darkness, his face obscured but his presence unmistakably familiar.

Her eyes snapped open, her breath coming in ragged gasps. The medallion felt hot in her hand, its glow fading as the vision dissipated. She looked up at the stranger, her voice trembling.

"There's someone else," she said. "Someone tied to the prophecy. He… he's part of this, but I don't know how."

The stranger's posture stiffened, his hands curling into fists. "What did you see?"

"Shadows," she said. "And him. He was cloaked, hidden, but I felt his presence. It was… familiar."

Before the stranger could respond, a loud crash shattered the stillness. The chapel door burst open, the wooden planks splintering as armed figures flooded inside. Their uniforms were black, adorned with the insignia of the Watchers—a star encircled by jagged lines. Ellara scrambled to her feet, clutching the medallion as fear surged through her.

The stranger drew his blade in one fluid motion, placing himself between Ellara and the intruders. "Stay behind me," he ordered, his voice cold and sharp.

The leader of the Watchers stepped forward, his face partially hidden by a hood. His piercing gaze locked onto Ellara, and a cruel smile spread across his lips. "The weaver and her guardian," he said mockingly. "How poetic."

"Leave her out of this," the stranger growled, his blade glinting in the lantern light. "You want me, don't you?"

The Watcher chuckled. "Oh, we want both of you. But you, my dear friend…" He pulled back his hood, revealing a face that made Ellara's blood run cold. "You've been a thorn in our side for far too long."

Ellara's breath hitched as she recognized him—the figure from her vision, the man cloaked in darkness. But here, his face was fully revealed, and her stomach churned with betrayal.

"Marcellus," the stranger spat, his voice laced with venom.

The Duke smirked, his icy blue eyes gleaming with malice. "You didn't think I'd let you play your little game unchecked, did you? This ends tonight."

Ellara's mind reeled. Marcellus had been hunting her all along, his words at the banquet nothing more than a prelude to this moment. She glanced at the stranger, whose grip on his blade tightened as he stepped forward.

"Run," he whispered to her. "Get out of here. I'll hold them off."

"I'm not leaving you," she said, her voice firm despite the fear coursing through her.

"You have to," he insisted. "You're the key to everything. If they take you, it's over."

Before she could argue further, Marcellus raised a hand, and the Watchers surged forward. The stranger met them head-on, his blade flashing in a blur of steel as he fought to keep them at bay. Ellara hesitated, her instincts screaming at her to flee, but her feet refused to move.

"Go!" the stranger shouted, his voice raw with urgency.

Tears stung her eyes as she turned and ran, clutching the medallion tightly. The sound of clashing swords and shouted orders followed her as she darted through the ruined chapel, her heart pounding in her chest.

She burst into the open air, the cold wind biting at her skin. The forest stretched out before her, its shadows deep and foreboding. But as she ran, a single thought burned in her mind.

The prophecy wasn't just a legacy—it was a curse. And now, betrayal had thrust her into the heart of its unraveling.

Ten

The Bond of Stars

The forest was a labyrinth of shadow and light as Ellara ran, the sound of her ragged breaths and the snapping of branches beneath her feet blending with the nocturnal symphony of the wilderness. The medallion clutched tightly in her hand pulsed faintly, its glow illuminating the darkness just enough to guide her path. Her legs burned with the effort of fleeing, but the memory of the betrayal she had just witnessed drove her forward.

Marcellus's face haunted her thoughts, his piercing blue eyes filled with malice as he revealed his true allegiance to the Watchers. The masked stranger's words echoed in her mind—"Run. You're the key to everything." But what good was being the key if she didn't even understand the lock?

The trees closed in around her, their gnarled branches clawing at her cloak like grasping fingers. Every sound—every rustle of leaves, every snap of a twig—sent her pulse racing. She knew the Watchers would be pursuing her. The only question was how much time she had left before they found her.

The forest floor sloped upward, and Ellara stumbled as her foot caught on an exposed root. She cried out as she fell, the medallion slipping from her grasp and landing in the dirt. Panic surged through her as she scrambled to retrieve it, her fingers fumbling with the smooth metal. As her hand closed around it, a sharp pain shot through her ankle—a cruel reminder of the injury she had sustained earlier.

She forced herself to her feet, biting back tears as she pressed onward. The slope leveled out into a small clearing, its center dominated by a pool of water so still it mirrored the stars above. The air here felt different—calmer, heavier with meaning. The clearing was bathed in moonlight, the silver glow lending it an almost ethereal quality.

Ellara hesitated at the edge of the pool, her breaths coming in short, uneven gasps. The medallion in her hand grew warmer, its light intensifying as though responding to the presence of the pool. She sank to her knees at the water's edge, her reflection rippling as her tears dripped into the surface.

"What am I supposed to do?" she whispered, her voice breaking. "I'm not strong enough for this."

The wind stilled, and for a moment, the world seemed to hold its breath. Then, from the depths of the forest, a figure emerged.

Ellara tensed, her fingers tightening around the medallion as she prepared to flee. But as the figure stepped into the moonlight, her breath caught.

It was the masked stranger.

He was battered and bloodied, his cloak torn and his movements unsteady, but he was alive. Relief flooded through Ellara, and she surged to her feet, her pain forgotten as she rushed to his side.

"You're hurt," she said, her voice trembling as she helped him to the ground.

"It's nothing," he muttered, though the strain in his voice betrayed the lie. "Are you all right? Did they follow you?"

"I don't think so," she said, glancing nervously at the shadows beyond the clearing. "But we can't stay here. They'll find us."

The stranger shook his head, his hand reaching out to grasp her arm. "Wait. This place… it's safe. For now."

Ellara frowned, her gaze shifting back to the pool. "What is this place?"

"A sanctuary," he said. "The Pool of Stars. It's tied to the Starwoven Arch, a place where the threads of fate converge. It's why the medallion led you here."

She stared at him, her mind racing. "You knew about this? Why didn't you tell me?"

"There wasn't time," he said, his voice filled with regret. "And I didn't want to burden you with more than you could handle. But now…" He gestured toward the pool. "You need to use it."

Ellara hesitated, the weight of his words pressing down on her. "Use it? How?"

"Look into the water," he said. "It will show you the bonds that tie you to the stars, the truths you need to see."

She knelt at the edge of the pool, her reflection shimmering in the starlight. The medallion pulsed in her hand, its light growing brighter as she held it over the water. Slowly, she lowered it into the pool, and the surface began to ripple, the stars within twisting and swirling.

The water glowed, and Ellara felt a strange pull, as though the pool was drawing her in. Her vision blurred, and when it cleared, she was no longer in the clearing.

She stood in a vast expanse of starlight, the threads of fate weaving around her in intricate patterns. At the center of it all was a tapestry—a glowing web that seemed to pulse with life. As she approached, she saw herself woven into the fabric, her figure connected to countless others by threads of light.

But there was something wrong. Dark tendrils snaked through the tapestry, their inky blackness threatening to unravel the intricate patterns. At their center stood Marcellus, his hands reaching out to sever the threads that bound Ellara to the stars.

"No," she whispered, her voice shaking.

"You see now," came the masked stranger's voice, though she couldn't see him. "This is why you're so important. You're the weaver who can repair the threads, who can stop the darkness from consuming everything."

The weight of his words settled on her like a physical force. "But I don't know how," she said, her voice cracking. "I don't even understand what I'm supposed to do."

"You don't have to know everything," he said. "You just have to trust the stars—and yourself."

The tapestry shimmered, and Ellara felt a surge of energy flow through her. The medallion in her hand glowed brighter, its light piercing through the darkness. She reached out instinctively, her fingers brushing the threads. As she touched them, the darkness recoiled, retreating from the light.

When she opened her eyes, she was back in the clearing, the masked stranger watching her intently. The pool of water was calm once more, its surface reflecting the stars above.

"I saw it," she said, her voice barely above a whisper. "The tapestry. The threads. Marcellus is trying to destroy it."

"And you stopped him," the stranger said, his tone filled with quiet pride. "You took the first step."

Ellara looked at him, her fear giving way to determination. "What happens now?"

"Now," he said, rising unsteadily to his feet, "we prepare for what's to come. The Watchers won't stop, and Marcellus won't rest until he's severed every thread. But you're stronger than they realize. The bond you have with the stars—that's your greatest weapon."

As the first light of dawn crept over the horizon, Ellara felt a new sense of purpose take root within her. The journey ahead would be treacherous, but she was no longer the frightened girl running from her destiny.

She was the Starwoven Weaver. And she was ready to fight.

Eleven

The Dagger and the Dance

The palace ballroom was a hive of glittering opulence, every detail meticulously arranged to impress and intimidate. Chandeliers sparkled with a thousand flames, casting golden light over the polished marble floors. The air hummed with music, laughter, and the gentle clink of goblets, but beneath the gaiety lingered a tension that made Ellara's every nerve tingle.

She stood at the edge of the grand hall, draped in a gown of deep crimson silk that flowed like liquid fire. Her face was obscured by a delicate mask of black lace, its intricate design hinting at mystery but offering little true concealment. The masked stranger's voice echoed in her mind: "The only way to gather what we need is to play their game. Trust no one, but act as if you trust everyone."

The Dagger and the Dance

The dagger strapped to her thigh beneath the folds of her dress felt like a lifeline, its cold steel reassuring against her skin. The masked stranger had insisted she carry it, his eyes hard with warning. "This place is a viper's nest," he had said. "They smile, but their blades are always ready."

The Watchers were here; of that, she was certain. Their influence seeped into the air like smoke, invisible but suffocating. Somewhere among the crowd was Marcellus, his silver tongue no doubt weaving lies as deftly as a weaver at a loom. He would be watching her, perhaps already suspecting her presence. The thought made her blood run cold.

Ellara took a deep breath, forcing herself to move deeper into the throng. Nobles in glittering attire turned to greet her with polite smiles and veiled curiosity, their eyes lingering just a moment too long. She returned their smiles, her practiced courtesies masking the storm of anxiety brewing within her.

"You look lost."

The voice was smooth and familiar, sending a shiver down her spine. She turned to find Lord Tavian standing before her, his dark suit tailored to perfection and his black mask glinting faintly under the chandelier's light. His sharp eyes studied her intently, his lips curved in a faint, knowing smile.

"I'm not lost," Ellara replied, forcing a calmness she didn't feel. "Merely observing."

Tavian chuckled, the sound low and rich. "A wise choice.

Observation often reveals more than conversation in places like this."

She inclined her head, hoping the angle would obscure her unease. "And what have you observed tonight, my lord?"

"Many things," he said, his gaze unwavering. "But none more intriguing than you."

Ellara's pulse quickened. Tavian's tone was casual, almost flirtatious, but there was an undercurrent of something darker, something calculated. She felt as if she were a puzzle he was eager to solve.

"I'm flattered," she said, her voice steady despite the tightness in her chest. "But I'm hardly the most interesting person here."

"Perhaps not to most," Tavian replied, stepping closer. "But I've always had an eye for the unusual."

Ellara forced a laugh, though it felt brittle. "And what is it about me that you find so unusual, my lord?"

He tilted his head, his smile sharpening. "You carry yourself like someone accustomed to shadow, yet here you are, standing in the light. That's a rare thing."

Before she could respond, the music shifted, the orchestra launching into a lively waltz. Tavian extended a hand, his dark eyes glinting. "Dance with me."

Ellara hesitated, her instincts screaming at her to refuse. But declining would draw attention, and attention was the last thing she needed. Plastering on a smile, she placed her hand in his, allowing him to lead her onto the dance floor.

The moment they began to move, Ellara realized her mistake. Tavian's hold was firm but not oppressive, his steps precise and commanding. He guided her effortlessly through the crowd, the two of them weaving among the other dancers like threads in a tapestry. Yet beneath the surface of his polished demeanor lay a predator, and she felt like prey caught in his web.

"You're quite skilled," he remarked, his voice low enough to be lost in the music. "Not just in dancing, I suspect."

"I don't know what you mean," she said, though the lie tasted bitter on her tongue.

"Don't you?" His smile widened, though his eyes remained sharp. "You've been watching the room as much as I have. But unlike most here, you're not searching for gossip or alliances. You're looking for something—or someone."

Ellara's heart raced, but she kept her expression neutral. "You're very perceptive, my lord. Perhaps too perceptive."

He chuckled softly. "It's a dangerous thing to be noticed, isn't it?"

She met his gaze, her jaw tightening. "Only if you're hiding something."

For a moment, their steps faltered, the tension between them crackling like a storm ready to break. Then Tavian laughed, the sound light but laced with menace. "Indeed."

The waltz came to an end, and Tavian released her with a bow. "Thank you for indulging me," he said, his voice smooth as silk. "I look forward to our next conversation."

Ellara forced a smile, nodding as he disappeared into the crowd. Her hands trembled as she smoothed her dress, the dagger at her thigh a stark reminder of the danger she was in. Tavian had been testing her, of that she was certain. And she had the sinking feeling that she had revealed more than she intended.

She moved toward the edge of the ballroom, seeking the shadows where she could observe without being seen. Her gaze darted across the room, searching for Marcellus. But before she could spot him, a hand grabbed her arm, pulling her into an alcove hidden behind heavy velvet curtains.

She gasped, her hand instinctively going to the dagger, but stopped when she saw the masked stranger. His chest rose and fell with quick, shallow breaths, and a faint sheen of sweat glistened on his brow.

"What are you doing?" she whispered, her voice sharp.

"Saving you," he replied, his voice low and urgent. "Tavian is dangerous. He's one of them."

"I know," she said, her pulse still racing. "He's testing me."

"And you're playing into his hands," the stranger said, his tone harsh. "He's trying to confirm what he already suspects—that you're connected to the prophecy. If he does, you won't leave this ballroom alive."

Ellara's stomach churned. "What do I do?"

"You leave," he said. "Now."

She hesitated, her gaze flickering toward the ballroom. "What about Marcellus? We need answers."

"And you won't get them if you're dead," the stranger snapped. "Trust me, Ellara. This isn't the time."

Reluctantly, she nodded. The stranger led her through a side passage, the noise of the ballroom fading behind them. Her heart pounded as they navigated the palace's labyrinthine corridors, every shadow a potential threat.

When they finally emerged into the cool night air, Ellara felt a surge of relief. But it was short-lived. A soft voice cut through the stillness, stopping them in their tracks.

"Leaving so soon?"

They turned to see Tavian standing at the edge of the courtyard, his smile as sharp as a blade. His hand rested casually on the hilt of a dagger at his side, but his posture was anything but relaxed.

"I was just beginning to enjoy the game," he said, his eyes gleaming with malice. "Shall we continue?"

Ellara's hand went to her own dagger, her breath catching in her throat. The dance was over, but the real battle had just begun.

Twelve

The Fading Star

~~~~~

The moon hung low in the night sky, its pale light diffused by a veil of dark clouds that shrouded the forest in gloom. The once-vivid constellations that had guided Ellara now seemed muted, their light dim and uncertain. The chill in the air seeped through her cloak, wrapping her in an icy grip as she crouched low in the underbrush, her breaths shallow and rapid. Every muscle in her body was tense, her senses straining for any sound, any movement that might betray the presence of the Watchers.

The ambush had been swift and brutal. What was meant to be a covert meeting with an ally—a merchant who claimed to have information about Marcellus's plans—had turned into a deadly trap. Ellara and the masked stranger had barely escaped the chaos, but the cost had been high. Their contact was dead, and now the Watchers were closing in.

"We can't keep running," Ellara whispered, her voice trembling. Her fingers tightened around the starwoven medallion hanging from her neck, its faint glow barely visible in the darkness. "They'll find us eventually."

The masked stranger knelt beside her, his blade glinting faintly in the moonlight. Blood stained his cloak, a reminder of the skirmish they had just survived. He didn't respond immediately, his focus on the faint rustling sounds coming from the direction they had fled. When he finally spoke, his voice was grim.

"We're not running. We're regrouping."

"Regrouping where?" she asked, her frustration breaking through her fear. "We're alone, outnumbered, and—"

"And still alive," he interrupted, his tone sharp. His eyes, shadowed by the mask, locked onto hers. "We can't give them what they want, Ellara. If they take you, everything we've fought for will be lost."

Her anger deflated, replaced by the crushing weight of responsibility. She looked away, her gaze fixed on the forest floor. "I don't even know what they want."

"They want the prophecy destroyed," he said, his voice softer now. "And you are the key to it."

The words hung in the air, heavy and inescapable. Ellara knew he was right, but the burden of her role felt insurmountable. She was just a weaver—a girl who had lived a quiet life until fate had thrust her into a battle she didn't understand. And now, the stars that had once guided her seemed to falter, their light fading like dying embers.

The sound of a snapping twig jolted her from her thoughts. She froze, her heart pounding as she exchanged a glance with the stranger. He gestured for her to stay low, his hand tightening on his blade. The rustling grew louder, accompanied by the faint crunch of boots on leaves. The Watchers were close.

The stranger moved swiftly, his movements silent and deliberate as he disappeared into the shadows. Ellara's pulse quickened as she crouched lower, her fingers brushing the hilt of the dagger strapped to her thigh. She didn't know if she could fight, but she would defend herself if it came to that.

The first figure appeared, cloaked in black with a blade drawn. His face was obscured by a hood, but the insignia of the Watchers—a star encircled by jagged lines—gleamed on his chest. Ellara's breath caught as she realized how close he was, his footsteps carrying him toward her hiding spot.

A blur of movement erupted from the shadows. The masked stranger struck with precision, his blade flashing as he engaged the Watcher. The clash of steel shattered the stillness, the sound sharp and violent. Ellara stayed frozen, her instincts warring between fight and flight.

The Watcher fell, a choked gasp escaping him as he crumpled to the ground. The stranger turned to her, his expression obscured but his urgency clear. "Go!" he hissed. "There will be more."

Ellara hesitated, her legs refusing to move. "I can't leave you—"

"Ellara, go!" he barked, his voice breaking through her paralysis.

She forced herself to her feet, her movements clumsy and desperate as she ran deeper into the forest. Branches clawed at her, and the uneven ground threatened to trip her with every step, but she didn't dare slow down. The sound of pursuit echoed behind her—shouts, the clash of weapons, the unmistakable thud of boots.

Her lungs burned as she pushed herself onward, her mind racing. She needed a plan, a way to outmaneuver her pursuers. But the forest offered little in the way of sanctuary, its labyrinthine paths both a blessing and a curse.

A sudden flare of light ahead stopped her in her tracks. She ducked behind a tree, her heart hammering as she peeked around the trunk. A group of Watchers stood in a clearing, their torches casting eerie shadows on their hooded faces. At their center was a man she recognized all too well—Marcellus.

The Duke's presence sent a chill through her. His silver hair gleamed in the torchlight, his piercing eyes scanning the trees with predatory intent. He held a blade in one hand, its edge catching the light, while his other hand rested on the hilt of a dagger at his side. He exuded confidence, his posture relaxed but ready.

"Find her," he commanded, his voice cold and authoritative. "She won't get far."

The Fading Star

Ellara pressed herself against the tree, her breath catching in her throat. Panic surged through her as she realized the noose was tightening. She was surrounded, her options dwindling with every passing moment.

Her grip on the medallion tightened as she closed her eyes, willing herself to think. The stars had guided her before—could they guide her now? She focused on the faint warmth emanating from the medallion, its light pulsing in time with her heartbeat. The threads of fate, the bond she shared with the stars—it had to mean something.

A soft whisper brushed against her mind, a voice that was both familiar and foreign. "Trust the light, Ellara. Trust yourself."

She opened her eyes, a spark of determination igniting within her. If the stars had not abandoned her, then neither would she abandon herself. Slowly, she drew the dagger from its sheath, its weight reassuring in her hand. The medallion's light grew brighter, casting a faint glow around her.

Moving with newfound purpose, she skirted the edge of the clearing, her steps silent and deliberate. The Watchers were focused on Marcellus, their torches creating deep shadows that she used to her advantage. She needed to get closer, to find a way to disrupt their formation.

As she approached, she caught snippets of their conversation. Marcellus's voice was low and mocking. "She doesn't even understand the power she wields. It would be almost pitiable, if it weren't so dangerous."

"She won't escape," one of the Watchers said. "We'll ensure that."

Ellara's jaw tightened. They underestimated her, and she would use that to her advantage.

When she was close enough, she took a deep breath, steeling herself. Then, with a burst of speed, she darted forward, aiming for the nearest torchbearer. Her dagger struck true, the Watcher crumpling before he could cry out. The torch fell, extinguishing as it hit the ground.

The clearing erupted into chaos. Shouts filled the air as the Watchers scrambled to react, their torches swinging wildly. Ellara darted back into the shadows, her heart pounding as she used the confusion to her advantage.

Marcellus's voice rang out, sharp and furious. "Find her! Now!"

Ellara didn't wait to see what would happen next. She ran, her body fueled by adrenaline and determination. She didn't know where the path would lead her, but she trusted the stars—and herself—to guide her.

As she disappeared into the forest, the light of the medallion shone brighter than ever, a beacon of hope in the encroaching darkness.

Thirteen

The Silent Alliance

The air in the forest was heavy, thick with the scent of damp earth and pine, as Ellara pressed her back against a wide tree trunk. Her heart thundered in her chest, a deafening rhythm that echoed the frantic pace of her thoughts. Darkness surrounded her, broken only by the faint, silvery glow of her starwoven medallion, which pulsed weakly against her chest. She held her breath, listening intently for the sound of pursuit. The forest had grown eerily silent since she escaped the Watchers, the absence of sound more unsettling than their shouts.

She wasn't safe. She knew that much. The Watchers were relentless, and Marcellus had made it abundantly clear that he wouldn't stop until he had her. She clenched the dagger in her hand, its weight both a comfort and a reminder of the danger she faced.

A faint rustle of leaves to her left snapped her attention to the present. She crouched lower, her fingers tightening around the hilt of the dagger. Her pulse quickened as a shadowy figure emerged from the underbrush, moving with deliberate slowness. The figure's face was obscured by a dark hood, but their posture was relaxed, almost casual.

Ellara's instincts screamed at her to flee, but something about the figure's movements gave her pause. They didn't seem like a Watcher—there was no aggression, no urgency in their approach. Instead, they stopped several feet away, their hands raised in a gesture of peace.

"Ellara," the figure said, their voice low and steady. "I mean you no harm."

Her breath hitched. The voice was familiar, though she couldn't place it immediately. She rose slightly from her crouch, her dagger still poised to strike. "Who are you?" she demanded, her voice sharp.

The figure reached up and lowered their hood, revealing a young man with sharp features and piercing green eyes. His dark hair was tousled, and a faint scar ran along his jawline. He looked at her with a mixture of caution and urgency.

"My name is Kieran," he said. "I've been watching you."

Ellara's grip on the dagger tightened. "Watching me? That doesn't exactly make me trust you."

Kieran nodded, his expression grim. "I understand. But if I wanted to harm you, I would have done so already."

She didn't lower her weapon. "You haven't explained why you've been watching me."

"Because you're the Weaver," he said simply. "And I'm here to help."

Ellara froze. The title felt like a weight, a chain that bound her to the prophecy she barely understood. She studied Kieran's face, searching for signs of deceit, but his gaze was steady, unwavering.

"How do you know who I am?" she asked, her voice softer now.

"I've known for a long time," Kieran replied. "The stars told me."

Her eyes narrowed. "That's not an answer."

He sighed, running a hand through his hair. "Fair enough. I'm… not like the Watchers, but I've been close enough to them to know how they operate. I've heard their whispers about you, about what you're capable of. And I've seen what they'll do to stop you."

Ellara's stomach churned. "Then why would you help me? If you've been close to the Watchers, why should I trust you?"

"Because I've seen what they truly are," Kieran said, his voice tinged with bitterness. "They hide behind the guise of protecting the balance, but all they care about is control. They fear you because they can't control you."

The sincerity in his tone made Ellara falter. She wanted to believe him, to trust that someone else was on her side. But trust was a luxury she couldn't afford.

"Prove it," she said finally. "Prove you're not working with them."

Kieran hesitated, then reached into his cloak. Ellara tensed, ready to strike, but he moved slowly, deliberately. He pulled out a small, weathered notebook and held it out to her.

"What is this?" she asked, not lowering her dagger.

"Proof," he said. "It's a ledger of their operations—names, locations, strategies. Everything they've done to manipulate and destroy anyone who opposes them."

Ellara reached out cautiously, taking the notebook and flipping through its pages. The entries were written in a meticulous hand, detailing covert missions, bribes, and assassinations. Her stomach turned as she read the cold, calculated words.

"This is…" she began, but her voice trailed off. She looked up at Kieran, suspicion still lingering in her eyes. "Why do you have this?"

"Because I stole it," he said simply. "It's why I'm on the run, why the Watchers would kill me if they found me. And it's why I came to find you."

Ellara studied him, her instincts battling her reason. If what he said was true, then the ledger was a weapon—one that could expose the Watchers' lies and weaken their grip on the kingdom. But if he was lying, if this was some elaborate ruse, then taking the ledger would only tighten the noose around her neck.

"What do you want from me?" she asked, her voice steady despite the turmoil inside her.

"I want to stop them," Kieran said, his green eyes burning with intensity. "And I believe you're the only one who can. The Watchers have built their power on fear and lies, but the prophecy... it threatens everything they've built. That's why they're hunting you."

Ellara's gaze dropped to the medallion glowing faintly against her chest. The threads of fate had brought her here, to this moment. She didn't know if she could trust Kieran, but she couldn't ignore the truth in his words. The Watchers were relentless, and she couldn't fight them alone.

"Fine," she said, slipping the dagger back into its sheath. "But if you betray me—"

"I won't," Kieran interrupted, his voice firm. "I swear it."

She nodded, though her trust was far from complete. "We need to move. They'll be looking for both of us now."

"Agreed," he said. "There's a place nearby—a safehouse. We can regroup there."

Ellara followed him as he led the way through the forest, her mind racing. The ledger in her hands felt heavier with every step, a tangible reminder of the stakes. She didn't know what the next move would be, but one thing was clear: the alliance she had just forged was as fragile as the light of a fading star.

The journey to the safehouse was tense, every sound in the forest setting her on edge. Kieran moved with practiced ease, his movements silent and deliberate. When they finally reached the small, hidden cabin nestled in a grove of trees, Ellara felt a flicker of relief. The cabin was modest, its wooden walls weathered but sturdy. Inside, a small fire crackled in the hearth, casting a warm glow over the sparsely furnished space.

Kieran locked the door behind them and turned to her. "We'll be safe here for the night."

Ellara sank into a chair by the fire, her body aching from exhaustion. She opened the ledger again, her eyes scanning the pages for anything that might give her an edge. The names listed were unfamiliar, but the strategies and locations painted a picture of a vast, insidious network.

"Thank you," she said quietly, surprising herself.

Kieran looked at her, his expression softening. "For what?"

"For not killing me," she said, a faint smile tugging at her lips despite the tension.

He chuckled, the sound warm and unexpected. "The thought never crossed my mind."

For the first time in what felt like forever, Ellara allowed herself to relax, if only for a moment. But as the firelight danced on the walls, she couldn't shake the feeling that their alliance, fragile as it was, would be tested before the dawn.

The stars outside continued their slow march across the sky, their light steady but distant. And Ellara, caught between hope and fear, prepared herself for whatever shadows the next day would bring.

Fourteen

The Starborn Trials

The sky was streaked with gray as dawn broke over the mountains, casting long shadows across the desolate valley. Ellara stood at the edge of the jagged cliffs, her breath fogging in the frigid morning air. Below her, the landscape stretched into a barren expanse of rocks and crags, interspersed with glimmers of frost that clung stubbornly to the earth. In her hand, she clutched the starwoven medallion, its faint glow muted but steady—a beacon of hope that felt increasingly fragile.

Beside her, Kieran tightened the straps of his satchel, his green eyes scanning the horizon. His face was set with a grim determination, the scar along his jaw catching the pale light. They had barely rested since leaving the forest safehouse, their flight driven by a singular purpose: reaching the Starborn Sanctum, an ancient site hidden deep within the valley. The ledger Kieran had given her remained tucked safely in her cloak, its secrets burning in her mind. If the Watchers discovered its contents, the consequences would be catastrophic.

"This is it," Kieran said, breaking the silence. "The entrance is just beyond those rocks."

Ellara followed his gaze, her stomach twisting at the sight of the narrow path winding downward. The way was treacherous, the rocks slick with ice and the drop steep enough to make her head spin. She swallowed hard, forcing her fear aside.

"Are you sure about this?" she asked, her voice trembling despite her best efforts to sound steady.

"Not entirely," Kieran admitted, glancing at her. "But the Sanctum is our only chance. If the prophecy is real, then the answers you need are there."

The prophecy. It was a word that had come to dominate her every waking moment, a shadow that loomed over her even when she closed her eyes. The idea that her fate was intertwined with the stars, that she was somehow destined to reshape the threads of existence, still felt impossible. And yet, the weight of it pressed on her shoulders, urging her forward.

"Let's go," she said, gripping the medallion tightly. The faint pulse of its light seemed to reassure her, even as doubt gnawed at her resolve.

The descent was slow and grueling. The narrow path forced

them to move single file, and every step required careful footing. The wind whipped at them, carrying with it a bone-deep chill that seeped through their cloaks. Ellara's heart pounded as she glanced at the sheer drop beside her, her fear of falling battling with the urgency driving her forward.

When they finally reached the valley floor, the landscape seemed even more barren than before. The rocks were sharp and jagged, and the air felt heavy, as though the earth itself bore the weight of centuries of secrets. Ahead, nestled between two towering cliffs, was a dark opening—a cave mouth that yawned like the maw of some ancient beast.

Kieran stopped, his hand resting on the hilt of his dagger as he surveyed their surroundings. "This is it," he said. "The Starborn Sanctum."

Ellara stepped closer, her eyes fixed on the cave. The air around it seemed to shimmer faintly, as though the light bent and twisted in defiance of natural laws. Her pulse quickened, a mixture of awe and apprehension surging through her.

"What happens inside?" she asked.

Kieran's expression darkened. "The trials."

She frowned. "Trials?"

He nodded, his voice low. "The Sanctum doesn't just reveal its secrets to anyone. It tests those who enter, forcing them to confront their deepest fears, their darkest truths. If you succeed, the stars will grant you their guidance. If you fail…"

Ellara's throat tightened. "If I fail?"

Kieran didn't answer, but the look in his eyes spoke volumes. Failure wasn't an option.

Taking a deep breath, she stepped toward the cave. The medallion grew warmer against her palm, its glow intensifying as she neared the entrance. Kieran followed close behind, his footsteps steady despite the tension radiating from him.

The moment they crossed the threshold, the air changed. The temperature dropped sharply, and the faint sound of whispers filled the darkness, echoing off the walls. Ellara shivered, her breath visible in the cold. The cave seemed to stretch endlessly before them, the faint glow of the medallion their only source of light.

"Stay close," Kieran said, his voice barely above a whisper. "And whatever you see, remember—it isn't real."

Ellara nodded, though her heart pounded with fear. The whispers grew louder as they ventured deeper, forming fragmented words that seemed to come from all directions. She gripped the medallion tighter, its light flickering as though responding to her unease.

The first trial came without warning. The ground beneath them shifted, and a sudden burst of light blinded her. When her vision cleared, she found herself alone, the cave replaced by a scene from her past.

She was back in her childhood home, the simple cottage where she had grown up. The scent of fresh bread filled the air, and sunlight streamed through the windows. For a moment, it felt real, as though she had been transported back in time. But then she saw her parents, their faces twisted in pain as they argued.

"You can't hide it forever," her mother said, her voice sharp with anger.

"I'm protecting her," her father snapped. "She doesn't need to know."

Ellara's heart clenched as she watched them, their words cutting through her like shards of glass. She had always suspected there was more to her past than they had told her, but hearing it confirmed left her breathless.

"She deserves the truth," her mother said, her voice breaking. "The stars chose her. We can't deny it."

The stars. Even then, the prophecy had loomed over her, shaping her life in ways she hadn't understood. Ellara wanted to scream, to demand answers, but her voice refused to come. The scene dissolved into darkness, leaving her trembling.

The whispers returned, louder now, and she realized she was back in the cave. Kieran's voice cut through the noise. "Ellara! Are you all right?"

"I…" She struggled to find the words, her hands shaking. "I saw them. My parents. They… they knew."

Kieran placed a hand on her shoulder, his touch grounding her. "It's part of the trial. The Sanctum forces you to face what you fear most. It's trying to break you."

Ellara swallowed hard, forcing herself to breathe. "I won't let it."

The trials continued as they moved deeper into the Sanctum. Each one was more harrowing than the last, forcing Ellara to confront her guilt, her doubts, and her deepest insecurities. She saw visions of the people she had failed, the choices she had made, and the lives she had altered simply by existing. The weight of it all threatened to crush her, but each time, she found the strength to push forward.

Finally, they reached the heart of the Sanctum. The chamber was vast, its walls shimmering with patterns of light that moved like living threads. At its center was an ancient pedestal, atop which rested a glowing orb. The medallion in Ellara's hand pulsed in rhythm with the orb, their connection undeniable.

"This is it," Kieran said, his voice filled with awe. "The source of the Starborn's power."

Ellara approached the pedestal, her steps slow and deliberate. The orb's light seemed to reach out to her, wrapping her in a warm, reassuring glow. As she placed the medallion on the pedestal, a surge of energy coursed through her, and the threads of light on the walls converged, forming a tapestry that stretched across the chamber.

The tapestry depicted the prophecy—the Weaver standing at the center of a web of light, her hands guiding the threads. But the image was incomplete, its edges frayed and darkened.

"This is the truth," Ellara whispered, her voice filled with wonder. "The stars… they're waiting for me to finish it."

But as the light grew brighter, a shadow fell across the chamber. Ellara turned, her blood running cold as she saw Marcellus step into the room, his blade drawn and his eyes burning with triumph.

"You've come far," he said, his voice echoing through the chamber. "But it ends here, Weaver."

Ellara's grip tightened on her dagger as the light of the stars surrounded her, and she prepared to face the darkness head-on.

Fifteen

A Web of Lies

The chamber's light flickered like a heartbeat, pulsing in rhythm with the glowing orb at its center. The ancient threads of the tapestry woven across the walls shimmered faintly, their patterns whispering truths and secrets Ellara was only beginning to understand. But none of that mattered now.

Marcellus stood at the edge of the room, his blade glinting in the soft light. His silver hair caught the glow, but his eyes, sharp and predatory, were fixed solely on Ellara. Behind him, a group of Watchers filed into the chamber, their dark cloaks blending with the shadows. They moved with a chilling precision, their faces hidden by hoods marked with the star-encircled insignia of their order.

Ellara stepped back instinctively, her hand tightening around the dagger she had drawn from its sheath. Her heart thundered in her chest, each beat echoing in her ears. Beside her, Kieran stood tense, his own blade ready, though the odds were clearly against them.

"This is a sacred place," Ellara said, her voice steady despite the fear coursing through her. "You don't belong here."

Marcellus smirked, his lips curling in a way that made her stomach churn. "Sacred? Perhaps. But sacredness has no meaning to the Watchers. We exist to control what you cannot comprehend."

"You mean destroy," Kieran snapped, stepping forward. "You can't stand what you don't own, so you erase it."

Marcellus turned his cold gaze to Kieran, his smirk fading. "Ah, the traitor speaks. I'm almost impressed that you've managed to stay alive this long, Kieran. You always were resourceful."

"Enough," Ellara interjected, her voice ringing through the chamber. "What do you want, Marcellus?"

He shifted his attention back to her, his expression softening into something almost pitying. "What I've always wanted: balance. Stability. The prophecy you represent is chaos, Ellara. You would unravel everything we've built."

Ellara felt the weight of his words, but she refused to be swayed. "The prophecy isn't chaos," she said. "It's truth. And you're afraid of it because it exposes your lies."

Marcellus chuckled softly, the sound devoid of humor. "You see only what the stars allow you to see. You have no idea what you're tampering with."

"Then enlighten me," Ellara challenged, her voice rising. "What are you so desperate to keep hidden?"

Marcellus's smirk returned, his eyes glinting with malice. "If you insist."

He raised his free hand, and the Watchers behind him stepped forward. Two of them carried a large, flat object draped in black cloth. They set it down carefully on the chamber floor, and Marcellus approached it, his movements deliberate.

"This," he said, gesturing to the object, "is what your precious prophecy leads to."

With a flourish, he pulled the cloth away, revealing a mirror-like surface that shimmered with an unnatural light. The reflection within wasn't of the chamber but of a swirling void, its depths filled with writhing shadows and faintly glowing stars. The sight made Ellara's stomach twist.

"What is that?" she asked, her voice barely above a whisper.

Marcellus's smile widened. "A fragment of the tapestry beyond the stars. The same power you claim to wield, but unfiltered, uncontrolled. Do you see now? Your so-called legacy would tear open the fabric of reality itself."

Ellara shook her head, refusing to believe him. "You're lying. The stars would never—"

"The stars don't care," Marcellus interrupted, his voice cold and cutting. "They weave their threads without regard for the lives they destroy. That is why the Watchers exist—to ensure that their chaos doesn't consume us all."

"By killing anyone who opposes you?" Kieran shot back. "By silencing those who could challenge your control?"

Marcellus turned to him, his eyes narrowing. "Order demands sacrifice, Kieran. Something you never understood."

Ellara's mind raced as she processed his words. Could there be truth in what he was saying? The stars had guided her, yes, but they had also thrust her into a battle she hadn't chosen, a destiny she didn't fully understand. And yet, the way Marcellus spoke, the calculated malice in his tone, told her he was twisting the truth to serve his own ends.

"I won't let you manipulate me," she said, her voice firm. "The stars chose me for a reason. I won't let you destroy that."

Marcellus's expression darkened. "So be it."

With a sharp motion, he gestured to the Watchers, who advanced toward Ellara and Kieran. The chamber erupted into chaos as the fight began. Kieran moved like a shadow, his blade flashing as he engaged the nearest Watcher. Ellara's heart pounded as she dodged the swing of a sword, her dagger slicing through the air in defense.

The glow of the tapestry intensified, the threads of light pulsing erratically as the conflict raged. Ellara felt the medallion grow warm against her chest, its energy surging as if responding to her desperation. She focused on the nearest Watcher, her movements guided by an instinct she didn't fully understand. Her dagger struck true, and the figure crumpled to the ground.

"Ellara!" Kieran's voice called out, drawing her attention. He was locked in combat with two Watchers, his movements quick but strained. She ran to his side, her blade catching one of the attackers off guard. Together, they forced the remaining Watcher back, their breaths ragged as they turned to face Marcellus.

The Duke stood near the glowing mirror, his expression unreadable. "Impressive," he said, his tone laced with mockery. "But you're too late."

Ellara's eyes widened as she saw him raise his blade. He plunged it into the mirror, shattering its surface. The void within erupted outward, tendrils of shadow and light spilling into the chamber like living smoke. The energy crackled with an intensity that made the ground tremble.

"What have you done?" she demanded, her voice rising over the chaos.

Marcellus smiled, his expression triumphant. "I've shown you the truth."

The tendrils lashed out, striking the tapestry on the walls. The threads began to unravel, their light dimming as the void consumed them. Ellara felt a surge of panic as she realized what was happening. The prophecy, the stars, everything—it was all at risk of being destroyed.

"You have to stop this!" Kieran shouted, his voice filled with urgency.

Ellara didn't know how, but she knew he was right. She gripped the medallion tightly, its glow intensifying as she stepped toward the void. The tendrils recoiled as she approached, the medallion's light cutting through the darkness.

"Ellara, no!" Kieran called out, but she didn't stop.

The energy around her surged as she held the medallion high, its light merging with the remnants of the tapestry. The threads began to reweave themselves, the void shrinking as the stars pushed it back. The effort left her breathless, her limbs trembling with the strain.

Marcellus's expression twisted into one of rage as he realized what was happening. He lunged toward her, his blade raised, but Kieran intercepted him. The two clashed in a fierce exchange of blows, their movements a blur of steel and fury.

Ellara focused on the tapestry, pouring every ounce of her will into restoring it. The medallion's light grew blinding, the chamber filled with a brilliance that outshone the darkness. Finally, with one last surge of energy, the void collapsed, its tendrils retreating into the mirror before the surface sealed shut.

The chamber fell silent, the tapestry whole once more. Ellara collapsed to her knees, her body trembling with exhaustion. Kieran stood over Marcellus, his blade at the Duke's throat.

"It's over," Kieran said, his voice cold.

But as Ellara looked into Marcellus's eyes, she saw a flicker of something that made her blood run cold.

A web of lies was never so easily unraveled. This was only the beginning.

Sixteen

The Celestial Betrayal

The tapestry hummed faintly, its threads glimmering in the aftermath of the void's retreat. The chamber was eerily quiet, the stillness broken only by Ellara's labored breaths as she knelt on the cold stone floor. Her hands still clutched the starwoven medallion, its once-brilliant light now a dull glow, as if exhausted by the battle it had just endured.

Nearby, Kieran stood over Marcellus, his blade hovering inches from the Duke's throat. The Watchers who had accompanied him lay scattered around the chamber, their forms motionless. Kieran's green eyes burned with a fierce intensity, his jaw clenched as he pressed the tip of his dagger harder against Marcellus's neck.

"It's over," Kieran said, his voice low and taut with restrained anger. "You've lost."

Marcellus, despite his position, smirked. The faint curl of his lips sent a chill down Ellara's spine. He looked far too calm, far too sure of himself for someone who had just failed. "Lost?" he repeated, his voice laced with mockery. "You think I've lost?"

Kieran's grip on the dagger tightened, but Ellara raised a hand to stop him. "Wait," she said, her voice hoarse. "There's something he's not telling us."

Marcellus turned his piercing gaze to her, his expression one of amusement. "Very perceptive, Weaver. You've finally begun to see the threads."

Ellara struggled to her feet, her body aching from the exertion of restoring the tapestry. She took a step closer, her dagger still in hand. "If you have something to say, say it. No more games."

Marcellus laughed, a cold, mirthless sound that echoed through the chamber. "Games? Oh, my dear, this entire prophecy, your so-called destiny, is a game. A cruel one, orchestrated by forces far beyond your comprehension."

"Enough riddles," Kieran snapped, his blade pressing against Marcellus's skin. "Speak plainly, or I'll end this."

Marcellus didn't flinch. Instead, he tilted his head slightly, his smirk widening. "Go ahead, kill me. But if you do, you'll never uncover the truth. You'll never understand why the stars chose her—or why they're lying to her."

The weight of his words sent a shockwave through Ellara. Her grip on the medallion tightened as she felt the familiar pull of doubt creep into her mind. "What do you mean, lying?"

Marcellus's expression turned serious, his eyes gleaming with a mixture of pity and triumph. "The stars don't choose heroes, Ellara. They choose pawns. They weave their threads, orchestrating events not for balance or harmony, but for their own ends. You're nothing more than a tool in their design."

"That's not true," Ellara said, though her voice wavered. "The stars—"

"Did they tell you everything?" Marcellus interrupted, his voice cutting through her like a blade. "Did they reveal the cost of this prophecy? The lives it will consume, the chaos it will unleash? Or did they simply show you what you wanted to see?"

Ellara took a step back, her mind racing. She thought of the visions she'd seen, the cryptic whispers, the way the medallion seemed to guide her without explanation. Was Marcellus telling the truth? Had she been blind to the full scope of the prophecy's consequences?

"Don't listen to him," Kieran said, his voice firm. "He's trying to manipulate you."

"Am I?" Marcellus countered, his gaze locking onto Ellara. "Tell me, Weaver, have you ever questioned the stars? Or have you simply obeyed, trusting them without understanding their motives?"

The Celestial Betrayal

Ellara opened her mouth to respond, but no words came. The truth was, she hadn't questioned. She had followed blindly, driven by fear and necessity, clinging to the belief that the stars knew best. Now, doubt gnawed at her, threatening to unravel everything she had built her resolve upon.

"Enough," Kieran growled, his patience snapping. He raised his blade, but before he could strike, Marcellus moved.

With a sudden burst of speed, the Duke twisted, knocking Kieran's dagger aside. He surged to his feet, grabbing a fallen Watcher's sword and leveling it at Kieran. The two men clashed, their blades sparking as they collided. Ellara stumbled back, her pulse pounding as she watched the fight unfold.

Kieran moved with agility and precision, but Marcellus fought with the ferocity of someone who had nothing to lose. Their movements were a blur of steel and shadow, the clash of their weapons echoing through the chamber.

Ellara's gaze darted to the tapestry, its threads still shimmering faintly. The medallion in her hand pulsed weakly, as if urging her to act. She couldn't let Marcellus win, not when so much was at stake.

Gathering her courage, she stepped forward, her dagger raised. But before she could intervene, Marcellus struck a brutal blow, disarming Kieran and sending him crashing to the ground. The Duke turned to Ellara, his sword glinting ominously.

"You think you're strong enough to carry the weight of the

stars?" he said, his voice cold. "Let me show you the truth of your destiny."

He raised his free hand, and the chamber darkened. The threads of the tapestry twisted and warped, their light dimming as shadows consumed them. A vision erupted before her, vivid and terrible—a world unraveling, its people consumed by war and despair. At the center of it all was Ellara, her hands tangled in the threads, her face etched with anguish as the stars' power overwhelmed her.

"No," she whispered, her voice trembling. "That's not—"

"That is your future," Marcellus said, his voice triumphant. "You are the harbinger of chaos, Ellara. The stars have cursed you, not blessed you."

Ellara's knees buckled as the vision consumed her. Doubt and fear threatened to drown her, the weight of Marcellus's words crushing her spirit. But then, from the depths of her despair, a spark ignited.

The medallion in her hand grew warm, its light surging with a sudden intensity. The vision shattered, and the tapestry's threads began to reweave themselves, their glow returning brighter than before. The warmth spread through her, filling her with a strength she hadn't known she possessed.

"You're wrong," she said, her voice steady now. "The stars didn't curse me. They gave me the power to fight back."

Marcellus lunged toward her, his sword raised, but Ellara moved faster. She raised the medallion, its light exploding outward in a blinding burst. The energy struck Marcellus, sending him staggering back, his sword falling from his grasp.

As the light faded, the tapestry glowed with a radiant brilliance, its threads pulsing with life. The chamber seemed to hum with energy, the air alive with the power of the stars. Marcellus collapsed to his knees, his face twisted with rage and disbelief.

"You can't stop it," he hissed. "The stars will destroy you."

Ellara stepped closer, her gaze unwavering. "They don't control me. I control them."

With a final surge of strength, she raised the medallion high, its light enveloping the chamber. The Watchers vanished into the shadows, their forms dissolving as the tapestry's power consumed them. Marcellus's scream echoed through the chamber as he, too, was swallowed by the light.

When the glow faded, the chamber was still. Kieran pushed himself to his feet, his eyes wide as he looked at Ellara. "What just happened?"

"I claimed my destiny," she said, her voice resolute. "But the stars aren't finished with us yet."

As the tapestry shimmered in the background, Ellara knew that the battle was far from over. The threads of fate had been rewoven, but the web of lies that Marcellus had spun still lingered. And in the distance, the stars continued to whisper their secrets, their light guiding her toward an uncertain future.

Seventeen

The Starlight Refuge

The sun dipped below the horizon, leaving the sky bathed in hues of purple and indigo. The forest was a silent labyrinth, its trees stretching toward the heavens like sentinels, their skeletal branches silhouetted against the fading light. Ellara trudged forward, her body weary but her mind sharp with the tension of pursuit. Behind her, Kieran moved with calculated precision, his blade drawn, eyes scanning the shadows for any sign of danger.

They had been running for hours. The Watchers' attack on the sanctuary had left them battered and exposed, their fragile alliance with the rebels shattered. The few who survived had scattered into the wilderness, leaving Ellara and Kieran to fend for themselves. The medallion around her neck pulsed faintly, its light dim and flickering like a dying star. It had guided them to safety before, but now its power seemed almost reluctant, as though it, too, was succumbing to exhaustion.

"Are you sure we're going the right way?" Kieran asked, his voice low but edged with urgency.

Ellara glanced at him, her fingers brushing the medallion. "I don't know," she admitted. "But this is the only path it's showing me."

Kieran frowned, his gaze shifting to the forest around them. "If the Watchers catch up to us, we won't have another chance to run. We need to find cover—soon."

As if in response to his words, the medallion grew warm against Ellara's skin. Its light flared briefly, casting a soft glow that illuminated the path ahead. A narrow trail wound through the trees, its end shrouded in mist. The air grew colder, and the faint sound of rushing water reached their ears.

"There," Ellara said, pointing to the trail. "It's leading us somewhere."

Kieran hesitated, his instincts warning against venturing into the unknown. But he trusted Ellara, and the urgency in her voice left little room for argument. With a nod, he followed her down the path, their steps careful but swift.

The trail opened into a secluded glade, its center dominated by a cascading waterfall that spilled into a crystalline pool. The water shimmered faintly, its surface reflecting the light of the stars that had begun to emerge overhead. The air here felt different—thicker, charged with an energy that seemed to hum just beneath the surface.

Ellara stopped at the edge of the pool, her breath catching as she took in the scene. The medallion's glow grew steadier, its warmth spreading through her chest. She knelt by the water, her fingers brushing its surface. It was icy cold but carried a strange vitality, as though it were alive.

"This place..." she murmured, her voice barely audible. "It feels... ancient."

Kieran stood behind her, his blade still in hand. His eyes scanned the glade, his every sense on high alert. "It's quiet. Too quiet."

Ellara ignored his unease, her focus on the medallion. Its light pulsed in rhythm with the waterfall, as though the two were connected. She closed her eyes, letting the sound of rushing water fill her mind. Slowly, a vision began to take shape—a faint image of a structure hidden behind the falls, its form shimmering like the threads of the tapestry.

"There's something here," she said, opening her eyes. "Behind the waterfall."

Kieran looked skeptical, but he trusted her judgment. "Stay

close," he said, stepping toward the falls. The spray from the water soaked his cloak as he moved cautiously, his blade raised in case of ambush. Ellara followed, her heart pounding as they approached the cascading wall of water.

Kieran reached out, his hand brushing the waterfall. His fingers met something solid—smooth, cold stone hidden behind the torrent. He pushed harder, and the water parted just enough to reveal a narrow entrance carved into the rock.

"This must be it," he said, turning to Ellara. "Are you ready?"

Ellara nodded, though her stomach churned with anticipation. Together, they stepped through the entrance, the sound of the waterfall fading as they moved deeper into the cavern beyond.

The cavern was dark and damp, its walls glistening with moisture. The faint light of the medallion illuminated the way, casting eerie shadows that danced along the stone. The air was heavy with the scent of moss and earth, and the sound of their footsteps echoed unnervingly.

As they ventured further, the passage widened into a vast chamber. The ceiling arched high above them, its surface dotted with tiny crystals that glowed faintly, mimicking the stars outside. At the center of the chamber stood a pedestal, its surface etched with intricate patterns that seemed to shift and shimmer in the dim light.

Ellara approached the pedestal, her breath catching as she realized what it was. The patterns were identical to the ones she had seen in the celestial tapestry, their lines weaving and intertwining in a dance of light and shadow. She placed the medallion on the pedestal, and the room came alive.

The crystals on the ceiling flared with light, casting the chamber in a soft glow. Threads of light emerged from the

The Starlight Refuge

pedestal, weaving themselves into a smaller, localized tapestry that hovered in the air. The threads pulsed with energy, their movements deliberate and purposeful.

Kieran stepped back, his eyes wide. "What is this place?"

Ellara reached out, her fingers brushing the threads. A surge of energy coursed through her, and images flooded her mind—visions of the past, the present, and possible futures. She saw the Watchers rising to power, their influence spreading like a disease. She saw the tapestry fraying, its threads pulled apart by greed and fear. And she saw herself, standing at the center of it all, the medallion in her hand.

"This is the Starlight Refuge," she said, her voice filled with awe. "It's where the Weavers before me came to understand their purpose. It's where I'll find the answers I need."

Kieran frowned, his unease growing. "Answers to what?"

Ellara turned to him, her eyes glowing faintly with the tapestry's light. "To how we stop the Watchers. To how we rebuild what's been broken."

Before Kieran could respond, the chamber trembled. The light of the tapestry flickered, and the shadows at the edges of the room began to writhe. A low, guttural growl echoed through the cavern, sending a chill down Ellara's spine.

"They've found us," Kieran said, his blade flashing as he stepped in front of her. "We need to move. Now."

The shadows coalesced into dark, humanoid forms, their glowing eyes fixed on Ellara. The Watchers had followed them, and they were no longer content to wait in the darkness. They surged forward, their movements silent but deadly.

Ellara raised the medallion, its light flaring as she focused on the tapestry. The threads responded, their energy weaving into a barrier that pushed the shadows back. But the Watchers were relentless, their strikes coming faster, more coordinated.

"Kieran, I need time!" she shouted, her voice echoing through the chamber.

"I'll give you as much as I can," he replied, his blade cutting through the advancing shadows. He moved with precision, each strike calculated, but the sheer number of enemies threatened to overwhelm him.

Ellara closed her eyes, her hands steady on the pedestal. She focused on the tapestry, letting its energy flow through her. The threads shifted and reformed, their patterns aligning into something new—a map, a guide to the power hidden within the Refuge.

The light of the tapestry flared brighter, and the shadows recoiled. The chamber trembled as the pedestal's energy surged, filling the room with a brilliance that drove the Watchers back. When the light faded, the shadows were gone, leaving only silence.

Kieran staggered to her side, his breathing heavy. "What did you do?"

Ellara looked at him, her expression resolute. "I unlocked the Refuge's power. We have what we need to fight back."

As the crystals above dimmed once more, Ellara knew their journey was far from over. The Watchers would return, stronger and more determined than ever. But for the first time, she felt a spark of hope. The Starlight Refuge had given them a chance—a weapon to turn the tide.

And she would use it.

Eighteen

The Prophecy Unraveled

The ancient sanctuary of the stars, hidden deep within the jagged cliffs of the Starlight Refuge, shimmered faintly under the glow of the celestial tapestry overhead. Threads of light danced across the chamber walls, their movements fluid and alive, as though they carried the weight of the universe's secrets. Ellara stood at the heart of it, the starwoven medallion resting against her chest, its glow matching the rhythmic pulse of the tapestry.

She felt the weight of the moment pressing on her. This was the culmination of everything—her journey, the battles, the betrayals, and the fragile alliances she had forged. She could feel the hum of power in the air, a resonance that stirred something deep within her soul. It was both exhilarating and terrifying.

Kieran stood beside her, his green eyes scanning the tapestry with a mixture of awe and trepidation. His hand rested on the hilt of his blade, a silent reminder of the dangers they had faced to reach this point. His voice broke the stillness, low and urgent.

"We don't have much time. The Watchers will regroup, and Marcellus's allies won't stop hunting us."

Ellara nodded, her gaze fixed on the glowing threads that wove and unraveled in an intricate dance. "I know. But this is the only way to end it."

Kieran hesitated, his expression darkening. "You've seen what the stars can do. Are you sure we can trust them?"

Ellara's hand brushed the medallion, its warmth grounding her. "I don't know," she admitted. "But if I don't try, the prophecy will consume everything. I have to understand what it truly means."

Taking a deep breath, she stepped closer to the tapestry. The threads seemed to respond to her presence, their movements becoming more deliberate, more focused. She reached out, her fingers brushing the glowing strands, and the world around her shifted.

—-

The sanctuary dissolved, replaced by a vast expanse of starlight. Ellara stood on a shimmering platform that seemed to stretch endlessly in all directions, the void around her alive with swirling constellations. The threads of the tapestry arced and looped across the space, forming a labyrinth of light that pulsed with a rhythm that matched her heartbeat.

"You have come far, Weaver."

The voice was soft yet commanding, echoing from everywhere and nowhere at once. Ellara turned, searching for its source, and her breath caught when a figure emerged from the starlight. The figure was cloaked in a gown of flowing light, their face obscured but their presence unmistakably powerful.

"Who are you?" Ellara asked, her voice trembling.

"I am the Keeper of the Threads," the figure replied. "I guard the truths of the stars and guide those chosen by their light. You are the first Weaver to stand here in centuries."

Ellara's heart pounded as she took a step forward. "Why me? Why was I chosen?"

The Keeper tilted their head, the light around them flickering. "Because you hold the will to shape the threads, to mend what is broken and challenge what must be undone. But you must understand—this power comes at a cost."

Ellara's stomach twisted. "What cost?"

The Keeper raised a hand, and the threads around them shifted. Scenes unfolded within the glowing strands—visions of kingdoms rising and falling, of battles fought and lives lost.

At the center of it all was Ellara, her hands guiding the threads as they wove themselves into intricate patterns.

"This is the prophecy," the Keeper said. "A cycle of creation and destruction, of balance and chaos. The stars chose you not to save the world, but to unmake it."

Ellara staggered back, her mind reeling. "Unmake it? What are you saying?"

"The tapestry you see before you is flawed," the Keeper explained. "The stars have woven a pattern that cannot sustain itself. To protect the balance, it must be unraveled and remade."

Ellara's chest tightened. "And I'm supposed to do that? Destroy everything?"

The Keeper's voice softened. "Not destroy. Transform. But to do so, you must make a choice."

The threads around Ellara shifted again, forming two distinct patterns. One depicted a world consumed by chaos, its people suffering as the threads unraveled. The other showed a new tapestry, its threads vibrant and strong, but its creation came at the cost of the old world's destruction.

"You can preserve what exists, knowing it will ultimately collapse," the Keeper said. "Or you can break the cycle, unravel the tapestry, and weave a new one. The choice is yours."

Ellara's hands trembled as she stared at the two patterns. The weight of the decision pressed down on her, threatening to crush her. She thought of the people she had met, the lives that would be affected by her choice. She thought of Kieran, who had risked everything to stand by her side. And she thought of Marcellus's words, his warnings about the stars and their true intentions.

"How do I know this isn't another manipulation?" she asked, her voice cracking. "How do I know I can trust you?"

The Keeper was silent for a moment, the light around them dimming. "You cannot," they said finally. "The stars are not infallible, and neither am I. But the threads do not lie. They show only what is, and what could be."

Ellara's gaze shifted to the medallion in her hand. Its light was steady, unwavering, as though urging her forward. She closed her eyes, letting the warmth seep into her, and allowed herself to feel the threads around her—not as abstract patterns, but as lives, stories, and choices woven together.

When she opened her eyes, her decision was made.

—-

The starlit void faded, and Ellara found herself back in the sanctuary. The tapestry glowed brighter than ever, its threads vibrating with an intensity that filled the air with a low hum. Kieran stood nearby, his expression filled with concern as he took in the determined set of her jaw.

"What happened?" he asked.

"I understand now," Ellara said, her voice steady. "The prophecy isn't about destruction. It's about change. The stars chose me to break the cycle, to weave something new."

Kieran's brow furrowed. "And what does that mean for us? For the world?"

Ellara hesitated, the weight of her choice settling on her shoulders. "It means everything will change. But we have to fight for it, to make sure the new tapestry is stronger than the one before."

Before Kieran could respond, the sanctuary trembled. The light of the tapestry flickered, and a cold wind swept through the chamber. Ellara turned to see the shadows of the Watchers gathering at the edges of the room, their forms twisting and writhing like living smoke.

"They're here," Kieran said, drawing his blade.

Ellara stepped forward, the medallion in her hand glowing with renewed strength. The threads of the tapestry seemed to pulse in time with her movements, their light pushing back the encroaching darkness.

"This is our chance," she said, her voice resolute. "We end this now."

As the Watchers advanced, Ellara reached out to the tapestry, her fingers brushing the glowing threads. The sanctuary erupted in light, and the battle for the future of the stars began.

Nineteen

The Starwoven Crown

The air in the sanctuary was electric, charged with the tension of what was to come. The glowing threads of the celestial tapestry stretched across the chamber, their light fluctuating like a heartbeat. Ellara stood at its center, the starwoven medallion clutched tightly in her hand. Its warmth seeped into her skin, a steady reminder of the power she carried—a power that both exhilarated and terrified her.

The Watchers, shadowy figures wreathed in darkness, moved closer, their presence distorting the air around them. Their leader, Marcellus, emerged from the shadows, his silver hair gleaming faintly in the tapestry's light. His piercing gaze was fixed on Ellara, his expression unreadable but his stance radiating menace.

"Do you feel it, Weaver?" Marcellus said, his voice cutting

through the charged silence. "The weight of the stars pressing down on you? This is the moment they've been guiding you toward. But do you even know what they're asking of you?"

Ellara's jaw tightened as she met his gaze. "I know enough," she said. "Enough to see through your lies."

Marcellus chuckled, a cold, mirthless sound. "My lies? The stars are the ones who have lied to you, Ellara. They've shown you glimpses of power, of destiny, but they've hidden the cost. Do you truly believe you can wield their crown without breaking under its weight?"

Her hand instinctively brushed the medallion, its glow steady and reassuring. "I won't let fear stop me. I'll protect the tapestry and the people it binds."

"Protect them?" Marcellus sneered. "You don't understand. The tapestry isn't salvation—it's a prison. It traps us all in its endless cycles of chaos and order. If you claim the Starwoven Crown, you won't free anyone. You'll simply become the new jailer."

His words sent a chill through Ellara, but she forced herself to stand firm. She couldn't afford to falter now. The threads of the tapestry pulsed in time with her heartbeat, as if urging her forward.

"I won't let you destroy this," she said, her voice steady. "The prophecy is mine to fulfill—not yours to twist."

Marcellus's smirk faded, replaced by a cold, calculating expression. He raised his hand, and the shadows around him surged forward, the Watchers advancing as one. Their movements were silent, but their intent was clear. Ellara's pulse quickened as she stepped back, her grip on the medallion tightening.

"Kieran!" she called, her voice sharp with urgency.

From the shadows behind her, Kieran emerged, his blade flashing in the tapestry's light. He positioned himself at her side, his green eyes blazing with determination. "I'm here," he said. "Whatever happens, we face it together."

The Watchers closed in, their dark forms swirling like smoke. Kieran struck first, his blade slicing through the nearest figure. The Watcher dissolved into shadow, but another took its place almost instantly. Ellara raised her dagger, her movements guided by instinct as she fought to keep the shadows at bay.

The sanctuary erupted into chaos, the clash of steel and the hiss of dissolving shadows filling the air. Ellara's movements became fluid, her body reacting faster than her mind could process. The medallion's light flared brighter with each strike, its energy coursing through her like a second heartbeat.

"Ellara, the tapestry!" Kieran shouted, parrying a blow from a Watcher. "They're trying to unravel it!"

Her gaze snapped to the celestial threads above. The Watchers' tendrils of darkness were reaching for the tapestry, their movements deliberate and calculated. The light of the threads flickered as the shadows touched them, their intricate patterns beginning to fray.

"No!" Ellara cried, surging toward the tapestry. She raised the medallion, its light blazing as she thrust it toward the fraying threads. The shadows recoiled, hissing as they dissolved in the medallion's glow.

Marcellus watched her from a distance, his expression calm, almost amused. "Do you see now, Weaver? The tapestry isn't unbreakable. It's fragile, like glass. And you're standing at its center, trying to hold it together with your bare hands."

Ellara ignored him, her focus on the tapestry. The medallion pulsed in her hand, its light seeping into the threads and weaving them back together. She could feel the energy of the stars flowing through her, a raw, untamed power that threatened to overwhelm her.

"Ellara, behind you!" Kieran's voice was a warning, but it came too late.

A shadowy tendril lashed out, striking her across the back. The force sent her sprawling to the ground, the medallion slipping from her grasp. Pain flared through her body as she struggled to push herself up. The Watchers loomed over her, their dark forms closing in.

"No!" Kieran shouted, his voice filled with panic. He fought his way toward her, but the shadows surrounded him, forcing him back.

The Starwoven Bride

Ellara reached for the medallion, her fingers brushing its edge. As her hand closed around it, a surge of energy erupted from the artifact, blasting the shadows away. She staggered to her feet, her body trembling but her resolve unbroken.

Marcellus stepped forward, his movements deliberate. In his hand, he held a blade of pure darkness, its edges shimmering with an unnatural light. "You're strong, Weaver," he said, his voice almost admiring. "Stronger than I expected. But strength alone won't save you."

He lunged at her, his blade slicing through the air. Ellara raised the medallion, its light clashing with the dark energy of his weapon. The force of the impact sent shockwaves through the chamber, the threads of the tapestry shuddering in response.

"You can't win, Marcellus," she said, her voice steady despite the strain. "The stars chose me, not you."

"The stars chose you to suffer," he spat. "Just like they chose me. We are their pawns, Ellara—nothing more."

Their blades clashed again, light and darkness intertwining in a deadly dance. Ellara could feel the medallion growing hotter in her hand, its energy building to a crescendo. She knew this was the moment, the choice she had to make.

As Marcellus lunged again, she sidestepped, raising the medallion high. Its light engulfed the chamber, brighter than ever before. The Watchers dissolved into the glow, their forms unraveling like threads in the wind. Marcellus staggered back, shielding his eyes from the brilliance.

Ellara turned to the tapestry, its threads still frayed but glowing with renewed strength. She could feel its pull, the connection between her and the stars stronger than ever. The medallion pulsed in her hand, its light merging with the tapestry's glow.

"This is my choice," she whispered, her voice filled with both fear and determination.

She thrust the medallion into the tapestry. The threads absorbed its light, their patterns shifting and reweaving into something new. The sanctuary trembled, the air alive with the power of the stars as the prophecy reached its culmination.

Marcellus's scream echoed through the chamber as he was consumed by the tapestry's light. The shadows dissolved, and the sanctuary fell silent.

Ellara collapsed to her knees, her body trembling with exhaustion. Kieran rushed to her side, his hands steadying her as she struggled to catch her breath.

"It's done," she said, her voice barely audible. "The tapestry is whole."

Kieran looked at her, his expression filled with a mixture of relief and awe. "You did it," he said. "You saved it."

But as Ellara looked at the tapestry, now glowing with a new and vibrant light, she couldn't shake the feeling that the battle wasn't truly over. The stars had given her their crown, but with it came a burden she wasn't sure she could bear.

And somewhere in the distance, a shadow watched, waiting for its chance to return.

Twenty

A Battle Under the Stars

The sky above the Starlight Refuge burned with the brilliance of a thousand stars. The tapestry, now whole, stretched across the heavens, its vibrant threads weaving a new and intricate pattern that pulsed with life. But beneath its glow, the ground trembled as a dark tide of shadows surged forward, heralding the arrival of the Watchers' army.

Ellara stood at the edge of the cliff, her breath forming clouds in the crisp night air. The starwoven medallion hung from her neck, its light steady and bright as it resonated with the tapestry above. Kieran stood beside her, his blade drawn and his stance tense. Around them, the few allies they had managed to gather—rebels, survivors, and defectors from the Watchers—prepared for what was to come.

"They'll be here soon," Kieran said, his voice low but steady.

"Marcellus might be gone, but the Watchers won't stop until they've torn the tapestry apart."

Ellara nodded, her gaze fixed on the horizon where the shadows writhed like a living sea. She could feel the medallion's energy coursing through her, a connection to the stars that both empowered and burdened her. She knew this would be the final confrontation—the moment where the fate of the tapestry, and the world it bound, would be decided.

The air grew colder, the wind carrying with it the faint whispers of the Watchers' approach. Ellara turned to her allies, her voice firm despite the fear that gnawed at her. "This isn't just about the prophecy. It's about our freedom. The Watchers have controlled us for too long, twisting the threads of fate to serve their own ends. Tonight, we take that power back."

A murmur of agreement rippled through the group, their faces grim but resolute. Kieran stepped forward, his green eyes blazing with determination. "We stand with you, Ellara. Whatever happens, we'll fight."

The ground shuddered as the shadows surged closer, their forms solidifying into twisted, humanoid figures. The Watchers' army was a nightmarish sight, their soldiers cloaked in darkness and wielding weapons that seemed to shimmer with unnatural energy. At their forefront was a figure unlike the others—a towering being of shadow and starlight, its form shifting and warping as it moved.

"That's not just a Watcher," Kieran said, his voice tight with alarm. "That's something else."

Ellara felt a chill run down her spine as she stared at the figure. It exuded a power that made the air feel heavy, its presence a dark counterpoint to the tapestry's light. She gripped the medallion tightly, its warmth steadying her.

"They're coming," she said, her voice steady. "Get ready."

The Watchers' army advanced, their movements eerily silent despite their numbers. Ellara's allies formed a defensive line, their weapons glinting in the starlight. Kieran took his place beside her, his blade raised and his expression resolute.

The first clash came with terrifying speed. The Watchers charged, their forms flowing like liquid shadow as they struck with blinding precision. Ellara's allies fought back, their cries echoing through the night as blades met darkness. The battlefield erupted into chaos, the light of the tapestry clashing with the Watchers' darkness in a violent storm.

Ellara raised the medallion, its light flaring as she focused on the tapestry above. The threads responded to her will, their glow intensifying as they wove themselves into barriers of light that repelled the Watchers' advance. But the shadows were relentless, their attacks growing more coordinated as the towering figure at their center directed them with precise gestures.

Kieran fought beside her, his movements swift and deadly. He parried a strike from a Watcher, his blade slicing through its form and sending it dissolving into mist. "Ellara, focus on the leader!" he shouted. "The others won't stop as long as it's controlling them!"

She nodded, her gaze locking onto the towering figure. The medallion's light flared brighter as she stepped forward, the energy of the stars surging through her. The figure turned to face her, its form shifting into something more defined—a humanoid shape cloaked in robes of shimmering darkness, its face obscured by a mask of shadow.

"You are bold, Weaver," the figure said, its voice resonating like a chorus of whispers. "But boldness alone will not save you."

Ellara gritted her teeth, the medallion's warmth steadying her. "I don't need saving. I'm here to stop you."

The figure laughed, a sound that echoed with malice. "You think you can undo what has been woven? The tapestry belongs to us. You are nothing more than a fleeting thread."

It raised a hand, and a surge of dark energy shot toward her. Ellara raised the medallion, its light flaring as it absorbed the attack. The energy dissipated, but the force of it sent her stumbling back. She gritted her teeth, focusing on the tapestry above.

"Help me," she whispered, her voice trembling. "Show me what to do."

The threads of the tapestry shifted, their patterns aligning into a new formation. Ellara felt the medallion grow hotter, its light surging as the tapestry's energy poured into her. She raised her hand, and the light erupted outward, forming a barrier that drove back the Watchers and their leader.

The towering figure hissed, its form rippling with rage. "You meddle with forces beyond your understanding. This will be your undoing."

It raised both hands, and the shadows around it surged upward, forming a massive spear of darkness. With a motion, it hurled the spear toward the tapestry, its intent clear—to pierce the threads and unravel everything.

"No!" Ellara cried, raising the medallion. The light erupted from her, forming a shield that intercepted the spear. The impact sent a shockwave through the battlefield, the ground trembling as the light and darkness clashed.

The spear dissolved, but the force of the attack left Ellara drained. She fell to one knee, her breaths ragged as she clutched the medallion. The towering figure advanced, its movements deliberate and menacing.

"Ellara!" Kieran shouted, rushing to her side. He stood between her and the figure, his blade raised. "You're not taking her!"

The figure laughed, the sound echoing with malice. "Foolish mortal. You cannot protect her."

Ellara forced herself to stand, her body trembling with exhaustion. She placed a hand on Kieran's shoulder, her gaze fixed on the figure. "We do this together," she said, her voice steady despite her fear.

Kieran nodded, his green eyes meeting hers. "Always."

The medallion's light flared brighter than ever, its energy merging with the threads of the tapestry. Ellara raised her hand, and the light coalesced into a massive wave that surged toward the figure. Kieran charged, his blade glowing with the tapestry's energy as he struck.

The figure screamed, its form unraveling as the light consumed it. The Watchers dissolved into mist, their army scattering as the tapestry's glow filled the battlefield. The ground trembled one last time before falling still, the silence almost deafening.

Ellara sank to her knees, the medallion's light fading as the tapestry returned to its steady glow. Kieran knelt beside her, his hand steadying her.

"It's over," he said, his voice soft.

Ellara looked at the tapestry, its threads vibrant and whole. "For now," she said, her voice filled with both relief and determination.

The stars above shimmered, their light a promise of the battles yet to come and the hope that would guide them.

Twenty-One

The Choice of Eternity

T he battlefield lay silent under the vast canopy of stars, the remnants of shadow dissipating like mist in the cool night air. The tapestry above shimmered, its light softer now, as if it were catching its breath after the ferocity of the battle. Ellara knelt at the heart of the Starlight Refuge, her fingers brushing the medallion that had guided her through every trial. Its glow was faint now, almost imperceptible, as though it, too, had spent its strength.

Kieran stood nearby, his blade sheathed and his face a mix of exhaustion and relief. He scanned the horizon, his green eyes sharp and alert despite the quiet. "The Watchers are gone," he said softly, his voice breaking the heavy silence. "At least for now."

Ellara nodded, though her heart was heavy. She had seen the

shadows retreat before, only to return stronger. Her gaze shifted to the celestial tapestry above, its threads weaving and shifting with a mesmerizing rhythm. She could feel its pull, a connection so deep it felt like a part of her soul. But beneath the awe was a lingering unease—the sense that her journey was not yet complete.

A low hum filled the air, vibrating through the ground beneath her feet. Ellara stiffened, her hand tightening around the medallion. The sound was soft at first, like a whisper, but it grew steadily louder until it resonated through the sanctuary. The tapestry's glow intensified, the threads pulsing with a light so brilliant it seemed to illuminate every corner of her mind.

Kieran took a step closer, his hand instinctively going to the hilt of his blade. "What's happening?"

Before Ellara could answer, the light from the tapestry descended, enveloping her in a cocoon of brilliance. She gasped as the world around her dissolved into starlight, her body weightless as she was pulled upward. Kieran's voice called out to her, but it was distant, muffled by the hum of the tapestry's power.

—-

When the light subsided, Ellara found herself standing on a platform of pure starlight. The vast expanse around her was filled with shimmering threads, each one connecting to the tapestry above. The stars glowed brighter here, their light weaving a path that seemed to stretch into eternity.

The Choice of Eternity

At the center of the platform stood a figure cloaked in robes of starlight, their form both ethereal and imposing. Their face was obscured, but their presence radiated authority and wisdom. Ellara instinctively clutched the medallion, its warmth a comforting anchor in the overwhelming brightness.

"Ellara, the Weaver," the figure said, their voice resonating like the harmony of a thousand stars. "You have come far. You stand at the threshold of eternity."

Ellara's throat tightened. She had faced countless dangers, battled shadows, and unraveled lies, but the weight of the figure's words made her feel small, insignificant in the face of the cosmos.

"Who are you?" she asked, her voice trembling.

"I am the Guardian of the Tapestry," the figure replied. "I exist to protect its balance and guide those who are chosen to shape it. You have been brought here to make the final choice."

Ellara's heart raced. "What choice?"

The Guardian extended a hand, and the threads around them shifted, forming two distinct patterns. One was vibrant and intricate, its colors vivid and its weave tight and orderly. The other was chaotic, its threads fraying and twisting, as though it were fighting against its own structure.

"These are the paths that lie before you," the Guardian said. "The first is to preserve the tapestry as it is, maintaining the balance that has existed for centuries. The threads will continue to bind the fates of all who live, but their freedom will remain constrained."

Ellara frowned, her mind racing. "And the second?"

"The second is to unravel the tapestry," the Guardian said, their voice tinged with gravity. "To free the threads from their bindings, allowing each one to weave its own path. It is the path of chaos, but also of true freedom. If you choose this, you will become the Crown of the Stars, the one who reshapes the cosmos."

Ellara's breath caught. She looked at the two patterns, their implications weighing heavily on her. "But… what happens to the people? What happens to their lives?"

The Guardian's gaze seemed to pierce through her. "If you preserve the tapestry, their lives will remain intertwined, their destinies guided by its threads. If you unravel it, they will forge their own paths, but the cost will be great. Entire realms may fall before new ones rise. This is the choice of eternity, Weaver. And it is yours alone to make."

Ellara's mind raced as she stared at the patterns. The first path was safe, familiar, but it felt like a cage. The second was terrifying, unpredictable, and yet it offered something she had longed for—freedom. But could she bear the responsibility of unmaking the world as it was?

"I don't know if I'm strong enough," she admitted, her voice barely above a whisper.

"You are," the Guardian said, their tone unwavering. "The stars would not have chosen you if they doubted your strength."

Ellara closed her eyes, her hand tightening around the medallion. She thought of the people she had met on her journey—their struggles, their hopes, and their fears. She thought of Kieran, who had stood by her side through every trial, and of Marcellus, whose twisted vision of order had nearly destroyed everything.

When she opened her eyes, her resolve was clear.

—-

The platform dissolved in a burst of light, and Ellara found herself back in the sanctuary. The tapestry above shimmered with an intensity that seemed to echo her decision. Kieran rushed to her side, his expression filled with relief and concern.

"Ellara! Are you all right? What happened?"

She turned to him, her gaze steady. "I've made my choice."

Before he could respond, the sanctuary trembled. The threads of the tapestry began to glow brighter, their patterns shifting as the medallion in Ellara's hand pulsed with power. She stepped forward, raising the medallion high.

"The stars gave us their light," she said, her voice strong. "But they also bound us to their will. I won't let that continue. It's time for us to choose our own destiny."

Kieran's eyes widened. "Ellara, are you sure? If you do this—"

"I'm sure," she said, her voice softening. "It's the only way."

The medallion flared with blinding light, and the tapestry responded, its threads unraveling in a cascade of brilliance. The sanctuary shook as the stars above seemed to shift, their light dancing wildly. Ellara felt the energy coursing through her, a force so vast it threatened to consume her.

As the last thread unraveled, the sanctuary fell silent. The tapestry was gone, its light replaced by an infinite expanse of stars. Ellara stood at the center, her body glowing faintly with the energy of the cosmos.

"It's done," she whispered, her voice filled with awe and sorrow.

Kieran stepped closer, his hand brushing hers. "What happens now?"

Ellara looked at him, her eyes shimmering with starlight. "Now, we build something new. Together."

The stars above shone brighter, their light no longer bound by the tapestry's design. And as the first rays of dawn broke over the horizon, Ellara felt a sense of hope she had never known. The future was unwritten, and for the first time, it was truly theirs to create.

Twenty-Two

The Starwoven Bride

The morning light broke over the horizon in a cascade of gold and amber, illuminating the ruins of the Starlight Refuge. The celestial tapestry was no more, its threads dissolved into the cosmos, leaving behind a sky that was vast and unbound. For the first time, the stars seemed distant, their light no longer pulsing with the rhythm of the tapestry's will but instead twinkling freely, as though sighing in relief.

Ellara stood in the heart of the sanctuary, the starwoven medallion resting heavily in her hands. Its glow had dimmed to a soft shimmer, a shadow of the brilliance it once held. She felt the weight of her choice settle fully now, the enormity of what she had done pressing on her shoulders. The tapestry was gone, and with it, the bindings that had controlled the lives of countless beings. The world was free, but freedom was never without cost.

Kieran approached her, his movements cautious as though he feared breaking the fragile stillness. His green eyes held a mixture of concern and admiration as he looked at her. "How do you feel?" he asked, his voice quiet.

Ellara took a deep breath, her gaze fixed on the medallion. "I don't know," she admitted. "It feels... empty. Like something is missing."

He nodded, stepping closer until he was standing by her side. "That's because it is. The tapestry was a part of everything. Even if we wanted to destroy it, it still bound us together."

Ellara's fingers tightened around the medallion as she turned to face him. "Do you think I made the right choice?"

Kieran's expression softened, and he placed a hand on her shoulder. "You made the only choice you could. It wasn't about right or wrong—it was about what you believed in. And I believe in you."

His words steadied her, but the doubts lingered at the edges of her mind. She had unraveled the very fabric of existence, set the threads free to weave their own paths. The freedom she had fought for felt precarious, like a fragile new dawn that could be extinguished at any moment.

"Ellara."

The voice was soft yet commanding, cutting through the quiet like the first note of a melody. She turned, her heart skipping a beat as a figure emerged from the shadows. It was the Guardian of the Tapestry, their form still cloaked in robes of starlight despite the tapestry's absence. Their face remained obscured, but their presence carried an undeniable weight.

"You have done what no Weaver before you dared to do," the Guardian said, their voice resonating like the hum of distant constellations. "You have unmade the threads of destiny."

Ellara's grip on the medallion tightened. "Was it the right thing to do?"

The Guardian tilted their head, their robes shifting like liquid light. "Right and wrong are not absolutes. The tapestry's destruction has brought freedom, but freedom is chaos. It is beauty and danger intertwined. What comes next is up to you."

"Up to me?" Ellara asked, her voice rising. "I've already made my choice. Isn't that enough?"

The Guardian's gaze seemed to pierce through her. "The choice was only the beginning. The tapestry may be gone, but the stars still burn. They will look to you for guidance, Ellara. You are the Starwoven Bride, the one who wedded herself to the cosmos. The fate of this world, and all worlds, rests in your hands."

Ellara's heart pounded, the weight of their words nearly overwhelming. "I didn't ask for this," she said, her voice trembling. "I just wanted to stop the Watchers, to free people from their control."

"And you have," the Guardian said. "But freedom is not the end. It is the start of something greater. The stars have chosen you, Ellara, not to bind the threads, but to weave something new."

Ellara looked at Kieran, searching his face for reassurance. He met her gaze, his expression steady. "Whatever comes next, you won't face it alone," he said. "We'll figure it out together."

The Guardian extended their hand, and the medallion in Ellara's grasp grew warm. Its light flared, casting long shadows across the sanctuary as it floated from her hand to hover between them.

"This medallion is a fragment of the tapestry's power," the Guardian said. "It is a key, a crown, and a compass. With it, you can weave new threads, create new patterns—but only if you embrace your role fully."

Ellara hesitated, the enormity of the decision making her knees weak. "And if I don't?" she asked, her voice barely above a whisper.

"Then the stars will drift, unmoored and untethered," the Guardian said. "The chaos will grow, and the balance you sought to restore will crumble. You must decide, Ellara—will you take the crown, or will you let the stars fall?"

The medallion pulsed, its light casting patterns of stars across her face. Ellara stared at it, her thoughts racing. She thought of the battles she had fought, the lives she had touched, and the people who had believed in her. She thought of the stars, their beauty and power, and the responsibility they carried. And she thought of Kieran, who had stood beside her through every trial.

"I'll do it," she said finally, her voice steady. "I'll take the crown. But not alone."

The Guardian inclined their head, their form flickering like the last embers of a fire. "You have chosen wisely, Starwoven Bride. The stars will guide you, but the path is yours to create."

The medallion flared one final time before settling back into Ellara's hands. Its light was steady now, warm and reassuring. The Guardian began to fade, their form dissolving into starlight that drifted upward to join the vast expanse above.

Ellara turned to Kieran, her gaze resolute. "This isn't the end," she said. "It's just the beginning."

He nodded, a faint smile playing at his lips. "Then let's make it a good one."

As the first light of dawn broke over the sanctuary, Ellara felt a strange sense of peace. The stars were no longer bound by the tapestry, but they were not lost. And neither was she. Together, they would weave a new destiny, one thread at a time.

www.ingramcontent.com/pod-product-compliance
Lightning Source LLC
LaVergne TN
LVHW021828060526
838201LV00058B/3559